Praise for *Do Less*

"In *Do Less*, Kate uses her signature, crystal clear wisdom to insist that we stop wearing busyness as a badge of honor and begin to claim our time, our peace, our lives. Then she shows us *how*. I inhaled *Do Less* and as I finished, I found myself breathing easier. Important book, perfect timing." — **Glennon Doyle, founder of Together Rising and author of #1** *New York Times* **bestseller** *Love Warrior*

"If you want off the 'I'm so busy/I'm so tired' train while making even more of an impact at work and at home, *this is your ticket*." — **Melissa Hartwig Urban, Whole30 co-founder and CEO,** *New York Times* **best-selling author, and single mom**

"*Do Less* had me from the very first page. Its message and method are game changers. Kate Northrup has written the new manifesto for how to claim your birthright of peace, health, and sanity in a world that teaches us just the opposite. This book is a must read for just about everyone." — **Christiane Northrup, M.D.,** *New York Times* **best-selling author of** *Women's Bodies, Women's Wisdom* **and** *Mother Daughter Wisdom*

"From the moment I opened up *Do Less*, my heart was put at ease. As a new mother, I am so grateful for the road map Kate lays out to make women more happy and full of joy." — **Vani Hari,** *New York Times* **best-selling author and founder of FoodBabe.com**

"As a recovering doer and as a psychiatrist who has witnessed the grave consequences of a life dictated by masculine principles of achievement, I will go so far as to say this book is essential reading for any woman in the feminine reclamation process." — **Kelly Brogan, M.D.,** *New York Times* **best-selling author of** *A Mind of Your Own*

"*Do Less* is here to help us honor our cyclical, nonlinear nature and redefine productivity. We're already wired with power and wisdom; rather than telling us what to do, Kate invites us to choose where to focus and when to rest, why to ask new questions, and how to nourish our intuition in order to arrive at the answers. Thank you, Kate, for this heartfelt, witty, and real map to doing less and loving more." — **Elena Brower, author of** *Practice You and Art of Attention*

"Kate Northrup's new book is a fabulous, paradigm-shifting guide for moms who are ready to bring rest and rhythms back into their lives—while thriving creatively and earning a living as well." — **Tara Mohr, author** *Playing Big: Practical Wisdom for Women Who Want to Speak Up, Create, and Lead*

"I inhaled this book because it illuminates a language about women and work that I've lived by without realizing it. I've never felt more validated or less alone in the way I do work as a woman in the world." — **Meggan Watterson, best-selling author of** *The Divine Feminine Oracle*

"Working moms need all the support they can get these days. This book is a practical, loving guide that helps women see their true worth, which changes the game for them financially, in relationships, and in every other facet of their lives." — **Farnoosh Torabi, best-selling author of** *When She Makes More* **and host of the** *So Money* **podcast**

"Kate Northrup has written one of the most relatable, current, and savvy books for this new era of womanhood. For every mom who is trying to do it all without doing herself in, Kate has provided you with a trustworthy loving road map: do less!" — **Kimberly Ann Johnson, author of** *The Fourth Trimester*

"The best way to describe *Do Less* is that it feels like a long, continuous, joyful exhale. I found myself nodding, and smiling, and even whispering an audible 'yes' while reading. I'm a mother-of-five and a hustler by nature, and what I hadn't realized before reading this book was how much I've been longing for permission to step back from that hustle. Kate lays out beautifully all the many ways we can be successful as nurturers while staying in total alignment with our natural rhythms (not in spite of them). *Do Less* is a gift to women." — **Rebekah Borucki, mother, author, and meditation guide**

"As a mother of three young girls I am thrilled this book is out. Kate has done a genius job of helping us honor ourselves so that we can honor the responsibility and the gift of mothering. I hope all mothers read this book." — **Patricia Moreno, founder of spiritual fitness, author of** *The IntenSati Method,* **and mom-of-three**

"*Do Less* is an invitation to a simpler, more peaceful life of discipline and abundance. I am a firm believer of 'being' above 'doing,' but sometimes the demands of the modern world make it challenging to manifest from a place of stillness. The blueprint that Kate lays out for success is clear, accessible, and easy to implement. Like an old friend who truly wants you to succeed, Kate speaks with transparency, generosity, and affection." — **Yaya DaCosta, actor**

"*Do Less* is a love letter to self. It is a gentle intervention and reminder that we are all enough. Kate's words on self-care and quality over quantity are a nurturing balm and an act of resistance all in one. *Do Less* is a handbook for those of us who are seeking to show up for our loved ones and for ourselves in the most fruitful and present way." — **Brandi Sellers-Jackson, creator of Not So Private Parts and birth and postpartum doula**

do less

Also by Kate Northrup

*Money: A Love Story: Untangle Your Financial Woes
and Create the Life You Really Want*

The above is available at your local bookstore,
or may be ordered by visiting:

Hay House USA: www.hayhouse.com®
Hay House Australia: www.hayhouse.com.au
Hay House UK: www.hayhouse.co.uk
Hay House India: www.hayhouse.co.in

● ● ●

do less

A **REVOLUTIONARY** Approach to Time and Energy Management for Busy Moms

kate northrup

HAY HOUSE, INC.
Carlsbad, California • New York City
London • Sydney • New Delhi

Published in the United States by: Hay House, Inc.: www.hayhouse.com®
Published in Australia by: Hay House Australia Pty. Ltd.: www.hayhouse.com.au
Published in the United Kingdom by: Hay House UK, Ltd.: www.hayhouse.co.uk
Published in India by: Hay House Publishers India: www.hayhouse.co.in

Cover design: Amy Grigoriou • *Interior design:* Bryn Starr Best
Interior graphics: © Freedom Family LLC

Cataloging-in-Publication Data is on file at the Library of Congress

Hardcover ISBN: 978-1-4019-5498-7
e-book ISBN: 978-1-4019-5500-7

10 9 8 7 6 5 4 3 2 1
1st edition, April 2019

Printed in the United States of America

For my daughters,

Penelope and Ruby.

May you always know

how valuable you are,

no matter what

you do.

contents

dive deeper
with
do less

While reading a book is the perfect way to start learning how to have more by doing less, you'll reap the profound benefits of this revolutionary approach to work and life only when you apply what you learn here!

I've crafted a special bundle of resources to support you in applying what you learn in this book, including a **community** to connect with other readers, a **guide** for going through the experiments with a group, a **cheat sheet** to all of the experiments, downloads of **planner pages**, and more!

You can get everything for free at www.katenorthrup .com/gifts.

foreword

I believe there are two new realities a mother faces upon foraying into parenthood. One of them is the actual *physical* reality of giving birth and having her body and life interminably alter themselves beyond recognition. The other is the *psychological* reality of now being responsible for another being. The pressure she faces from within is fierce; however, it pales in comparison to the pressure she faces from without. The force of culture bears down upon her with constant reminders from others of how she "should" be. Our society has a plethora of expectations for the new mother, demanding that she juggle a million tasks and outperform herself to exhaustion.

In fact, most women can relate to this ubiquitous dilemma: How can I give of myself while still attending to my genuine self-care? The "solution," too often, is ignoring our own care in favor of others'.

In my own adulthood and, later, motherhood, I remember feeling eternally distraught about the fact that I wasn't out saving the world or at least working at some high-powered corporate job. I had a constant gnawing sense that I needed to be doing *more* than I currently was—no matter what I was doing, I surely could be doing more and doing *better*. Motherhood's drastic transformations left me breathless and extremely anxious. If I wasn't being cajoled to have another child, I was being pressured to enroll my child in all sorts of activities, while also being reminded of the constant onus to look better or give more to my family. I remember saying to myself, "Am I only a stay-at-home mom? That's it?" I felt plagued by the idea that I was sacrificing my life in some way. At the same time, I felt that my early years home with my baby were priceless. I intuitively knew that I needed to "give" of myself in this way, not only for her sake but also for the purpose of my own internal spiritual growth.

The current parenting paradigm in our culture is that we women are expected to be all things for all people, placing ourselves last on the list. As a result, too many of us are fraught with a low sense of worth, as being a superwoman is simply unachievable. We feel like constant failures, constantly "lesser than." It is only when we women realize how culture places an inordinate burden of perfection and achievement on us that we will begin to break free from our psychological shackles. In my own experience, it was only when I began to undergo a tremendous personal process of healing and recovery that I was able to unshackle myself, one clasp at a time.

And this is the gift Kate Northrup offers us in this magnificent book: an opportunity for us women to uncage ourselves and free our authentic natures into the wild where they belong. Kate's poetic and strategic invitation reminds us of our true manifestation as daughters of Mother Earth, nestled within the rhythms and cycles of the seasons. She reminds us of the power of releasing the burdens of expectation from our shoulders so that we can place ourselves first in terms of self-care, self-worth, and, most important, self-compassion. It is only when we begin attuning to our inner sense of divinity that we can fully serve those we love. It all begins with a deconditioning of the old paradigms of *doing-more* in order to *be-of-worth* and entering a revolutionary way of flowing with one's true nature: *doing-less* in order to *be-more-yourself.*

Full of strategies and concrete tools, this book offers us women a valuable path of self-discovery, transformation, and transcendence. Kate teaches us about the power of intuition, our amazing physiologies, and, most crucially, our innate knowing. When we engage with abandon the exercises she offers us, we discover the courage to reprogram our entire existence. Now, productivity gets redefined and success gets reframed. A life well lived is no longer measured by a stack of achievements, but instead by a stack of presence-filled experiences. When we enter into this quiet but profound realization, our entire world shifts its axis. We no longer seek outer validation or outer worth. Now we tune within and rely on the seasons of the earth to guide us to our truth. And this time, because of all the inner work we have embarked on, we do so boldly and fiercely, ready to answer the call of the wild and free.

Kate's book is an ode to all women, creating a space for us to deeply explore our innate knowing and wisdom. She gently guides us on a journey back into our womb of great courage and daring authenticity. This book will help free many women to fly into the destinies they were born for.

— Dr. Shefali Tsabary
clinical psychologist and *New York Times* best-selling
author of *The Awakened Family*, www.drshefali.com

It is my intention for this book to be inclusive. It's incredibly important that you know that no matter your gender expression, parental status, sexual orientation, race, ethnicity, religious beliefs, education level, ability, class, body composition, or background, you matter and you are welcome here. I'm committed to continuing to do the work to uncover the unconscious bias that I harbor (because we all do) and I am always looking to do better. Thank you for being here with me on this journey.

introduction

We sat around our round dining room table, which was encrusted with little spots of glue and glitter left over from little girls' craft projects. I watched as my mother ceremoniously tied a red ribbon around my sister's head, letting the long ends fall down her back.

My sister was proud. My mom was proud.

I just felt uncomfortable.

My sister had gotten her period for the first time, and my mom was leading us in a celebration of this rite of passage. My dad had gotten her flowers on his way home from work. There was a special dinner prepared in honor of the big day.

Not that much later, I got my period for the first time. I was 12, and I was devastated. I told my mom she wasn't allowed to bless me. And for the love of God, please don't tell Dad.

It was not a day of celebration for me. It was a day of mourning. I lay in bed all day and cried. Then I figured out how to use tampons on my own because I was having a birthday party in a couple of days and I was not going to miss out on sitting around in the hot tub with my girlfriends.

I was raised by a major champion for women's bodies and the wisdom therein, Dr. Christiane Northrup. So what was up with my sadness for this pivotal moment of beginning the transition from girl to woman?

Even though I could never have articulated it at the time, I think I could sense that I was becoming a woman within a culture where the feminine, the very essence that makes us women, has been dishonored for the last 5,000 years. I think I was sad for all of my foremothers whose feminine wisdom hadn't been celebrated. And I subconsciously mourned for my future of growing up in a culture that made the natural cycles of women, the cycles responsible for life itself, a taboo.

Oh, don't talk about that: It's gross. It's not polite. Eeeeew. You're so weird.

I desperately wanted my mom to be like the other mothers. I just wanted her to be normal.

But I didn't get that. I was raised by a revolutionary. I was raised by a pioneer. And even though I wanted her to fit in, and I thought I wanted to fit in too, I'm glad we didn't.

Yes, I was raised by a woman who's written giant books about the wisdom of the female body and of the feminine at large. Honoring my menstrual cycle and everything about my body and my femininity should have come naturally to me—or should it have?

My mom worked her ass off while writing those books about honoring the feminine. She didn't sleep enough. She didn't rest enough. She was up every third night delivering babies for her entire adulthood until I was two years old.

Premed. Medical school. Residency. Fellowship. Pregnancy one. Baby one. (Deliver tons of babies in between.) Pregnancy two. Baby two. (Keep delivering tons of babies.)

She taught about the wisdom of the feminine to protect, nourish, and take care of our bodies, but she didn't live within a culture that allowed that to happen for her, and she certainly didn't choose a career that made that possible.

I witnessed both of my parents work, work, work, work, work, work, work my entire childhood. Productivity was a Holy Grail, sought against all odds. Doingness was next to godliness. I got my first Day-Timer planner when I was 14 years old and proudly began to schedule myself within an inch of my life.

I started my first businesses when my age was in the single digits, and I still run a business I began when I was only 18 years old.

I thought that productivity was what made us valuable. *Look at what I've done, and I'll show you how much I'm worth.*

• • •

The way we work in our culture is as though we're in a perpetual harvest. But anyone who's grown anything in the earth knows that this is impossible.

Our bodies are made of 60 percent water. Water is affected by the moon; that's what creates tides. Our bodies are affected by the moon too. In fact, it affects our hormonal cycles in miraculous ways. When women are living away from artificial light, our cycles automatically sync up with the lunar cycles, bleeding at the new moon and ovulating at the full moon.

Whether male or female, our bodies have cycles. These cycles take us through a literal or metaphorical preparation for fertilization and shedding each and every month. Yet we ask our bodies to be in production mode all the time. Yes, we are more than our bodies, but our days and what's possible energetically are governed by the fact that we each live in a body.

We are animals. We are nature. Yet we live and work as though we're not.

We ask for perpetual production, and yet this is impossible. When a seed is planted, it takes time, care, and resources before it sprouts and grows to its fullest expression. As humans, our creative process is no different, yet we've forgotten that we need time, care, and space to not only do our best work but also to show up as our best selves.

When you continue to plant the same crop in a field over and over and over again without ever giving it a break, the crops suffer as the soil degrades; eventually there is no harvest. The fruits and veggies we ate today have been proven to be less nutritious than the ones our grandparents were eating because of agricultural practices that focus on getting the biggest, most pest-resilient harvest as fast as possible instead of the highest-quality harvest.[1]

Not surprisingly, the way we raise fruits and vegetables is reflected in the way we produce everything. The focus is on getting the most impressive outcome the fastest without a lot of attention to quality or the long-term implications of how we get the result and how that affects the whole of humanity, our planet, and even the Universe.

Focus on quantity and growth above quality and sustainability leaves the soil depleted. Focus on these very same deliverables leaves humans depleted.

Stress, of which overwork is obviously a cause, has been correlated to depleted nutrients that help with hormone production and regulation, such as magnesium, zinc, and calcium. Once again: We are not separate from nature. We *are* nature and must treat ourselves as such.[2]

When we ask ourselves to work and produce and create and birth with no fallow time, we burn out. We become ill. Diseases like karoshi, a Japanese word that literally translates to "death by overwork," develop. Instead of nourishing life, which is what our bodies were designed to do, we work ourselves to death.

The feminine is rising; it's hard to ignore that. We're starting to understand that we need our intuitive, generous, and nurturing sides in order to thrive as a species. We are beginning to understand that life is not always linear, that there's beauty and value in the unknown, and that there's more to life than what we have to show for a day's work.

Women, especially mothers, are leaving the traditional workforce to start businesses, work freelance, and earn income in nontraditional ways because our traditional economic systems are not set up to support our lives and our thriving. As of 2014, 7 out of 10 mothers of children under the age of 18 are part of the labor force, many of them as freelancers within the "gig economy." One in three mothers of kids under six years old are employed part-time. In fact, female part-time earners make an average of $10 more weekly than their male counterparts.[3]

At the time of this writing, only five U.S. states—California, New Jersey, Rhode Island, Massachusetts, and New York— plus the District of Columbia offer any paid family leave at all. While this is a start, we still have a long way to go. Out of 41 countries in the Organization for Economic Cooperation and Development, the U.S. is the only one without mandated paid leave for new parents.[4]

Many women are simply choosing to opt out of the system altogether. The system was not created to support us optimally, so why stay there? It's better to sacrifice our careers and earn less (or nothing) but be able to create lives for and love our little people, right?

The typical corporate environment is still set up to work for someone who has significant support on the home front (aka a man with a wife at home) despite the fact that nearly half of two-parent households have both parents working, and in 40 percent of families, the mother is the primary breadwinner.[5]

In her book *Drop the Ball,* Tiffany Dufu astutely points out that in order for corporate and public policies to shift to support humans thriving by offering paid family leave, flexible hours, and more, we need more women in leadership positions deciding on the policies in the first place. She writes:

> There continues to be a dearth of women in top leadership positions, and the root of the problem is that the leadership pipeline for college-educated women breaks down at middle management. It is at this point in a professional career that energy expended at work needs to shift from a focus on performance to a focus on what it actually takes to get to the top. . . . Many women reach this point at the precise moment they're starting their families. . . . It's no wonder, then, that women represent 53 percent of corporate entry-level jobs but only 14 percent of the executive committee level. . . . The overwhelming majority of male executives—94.6 percent—are married with children, but only 46 percent of top corporate women are married, and only 52 percent of them are mothers.[6]

It's not an issue of "leaning in." Those who look at the stats of women leaving the workplace and think it's caused by a lack of assertiveness, direction, mentorship, and basically getting in there and getting what we want are completely missing the bigger picture.

The bigger picture is that the systems were created by men for men.

Women, however, innately know how to nurture life. Our bodies are designed to do it for nine months without us even having to have one conscious thought about how to do it. We know when we're operating within a system that doesn't support life. Women don't need to lean in to fix the system. We need to *lean out* so that the systems that don't support our well-being can collapse and new ones can be formed. And that's what we're doing . . . in droves.

Choosing our own models of navigating family and career that work for our own versions of success and satisfaction. Homeschooling while running an online business at home. Forming child-care co-ops so that we can share child care for free and each have some free time to work on our businesses at the kitchen table. Working part-time at a career we love so that we get to pursue our dreams but not miss our children's lives. Shifting the expectations and toppling traditional gender roles so that we have more support on the home front as we venture out to pursue our vocations.

Many of us, like me, have chosen never to enter the corporate system. Besides one "regular" job for four months where I worked in a tiny office in downtown New York City doing event planning, I've always opted out of the traditional system.

My community of blog subscribers and customers is primarily made up of "opt-outers." We get that we can't wait for the CEOs and the heads of state to get it that honoring the feminine, the very qualities that make life possible, is important. Paid family leave? Yeah! That would be awesome. But I'm not going to wait to have babies until some stodgy old guy in a suit finally gets it through his head that supporting me to do that is a good idea.

So we opt out. And we run our own show. We become freelancers. We work from home. We become stay-at-home moms. We start our own businesses. We create unusual scenarios of commerce so that we can support ourselves (or be financially supported) and also support life. But then we pull the same shit as if we were punching the clock at a typical corporate gig.

We expect ourselves to be in a perpetual late summer/ early autumn. We ask for the harvest year-round.

Our bodies ask us to take a break, and we feel guilty. We beat ourselves up for rest. We feel terrified to tell our families and communities when we don't know what's next in our careers or our lives because God forbid we fall off the linear path of success and take a detour into the fertile void of "I don't know."

We boldly opt out of the system to create one that works for us, and then we work ourselves to the bone, following the model that we wanted to escape in the first place.

The answer is not someone else passing a policy that allows us to work the way we want to. The answer is supporting it within ourselves, in our daily work lives, and in our homes.

Because the only way to create a new system is to *be* it.

● ● ●

When I got my first period since giving birth to my first daughter, for the first time in my life I was excited and not annoyed.

Yes, even me, the daughter of a women's health and wisdom pioneer. It's taken me a long time to come around to embracing the wisdom that resides within my monthly connection to the moon and my ability to gestate and birth life.

It took actually doing that to get just how awesome it is.

When I was 18, I got a vision for my life that I wanted to create financial freedom (enough residual income to cover my living expenses) by the age of 30 so that I could stay home with my kids one day.

Now I'm married with two young girls (a one-year-old and a preschooler at the time of publication) and my husband, Mike, and I do earn enough residual income that we could stop working for the most part and live a good life. But it wasn't long into motherhood that I realized that I'm a working mother, not a stay-at-home mother.

(A side note: I offer a deep bow to the women who lead on the home front as "stay-at-home mothers." Our society does not honor them enough! I love that Tiffany Dufu refers to this group as *nonpaid working mothers* instead because it's far more accurate. These women work. A lot. They simply don't get paid for it due to our cultural values being catty-wampus and the work of nurturing not being honored in the way it should be.)

I started getting the itch to go back to work when our daughter Penelope was about five weeks old. Yet the first year of motherhood didn't offer a lot of space and freedom to work on our business due to the physical and emotional demands that showing up for our baby required. I was working, just in a very different way than I'd ever been used to before.

I've never been so tired as when I was pregnant. Even after over a year of interrupted sleep nearly nightly and crack-of-dawn wake-ups ("Hi, Mom! It's 3 A.M.! Let's play!"), I'm still not as tired as I was while pregnant.

During my first trimester, I had friends tell me to wait until the second trimester because they'd felt huge energy surges then. One friend told me she wrote five book proposals during her second trimester. I awaited the surge.

Nothing came. I just felt tired. As my belly grew, the fatigue deepened. By the time I went on maternity leave, I had stopped working full-time. Beyond a few hours a week to fulfill the bare minimum (writing my weekly blog and a few marketing e-mails), I didn't do much that could be quantified as "productive." Yet it was the most productive year of my life. I made a human being.

Here's what's amazing to me, looking back:

As I've found is the case with a lot of families, the first year of parenthood was no walk in the park. Penelope is not only not much of a sleeper, she also developed severe eczema at four months old that covered her entire body and caused her to itch all night and all day, often waking every 10 minutes at night screaming. Between the stress of having a sick, miserable baby and all of the appointments seeing different practitioners to try to heal her eczema, Mike and I were both run ragged.

We had 10 hours a week of child care with a nanny in our home from when P was three months old to nine months old, and then she started day care three days a week. Basically from 2014 through 2016, the amount I worked was just about cut in half compared to the previous years of my adult life. And our business revenue remained steady.

In 2015 I worked far less than half the amount I'd worked in 2014, and probably only a quarter of the time I'd worked in 2013. 2016 was such a blur of sleep deprivation and doctor's appointments, I don't even really know what I did for work. And yet, during all this time, our income didn't suffer. We didn't grow our business, but it didn't tank. And I was pretty surprised.

This made me realize two things: (1) Much of what I'd been doing to keep myself busy prior to getting pregnant was unnecessary. (2) My power and worth go far beyond the list of things I'd accomplished by the end of a workday.

It was really the first time in my life that I'd allowed my body to dictate my schedule. She was speaking so loud to me as she grew our child that I couldn't ignore her and push through. For the first time, someone else's well-being (my baby's) depended on my physical well-being. I couldn't sacrifice my body for productivity anymore because I knew that pushing past my profound fatigue would ultimately be harmful for my baby. I finally understood what people mean when they say you need to take care of yourself so that you can fully show up for others.

I was in a season of gestation. It required nourishment, rest, and stillness. My body wouldn't let me do much more than the gentlest of movements. Even walking became painful as the pressure of the baby sat on my pelvis and affected my knees.

My creative juices were pretty much going to the baby. I didn't feel particularly inspired about my business. I didn't have any great ideas cooking. I just did the least amount I needed to do in order to keep things running.

Up until this time in my life, I thought that taking a real break would mean the business would collapse and revenue would end up in the toilet. What I found, though, was the complete opposite.

I found that as I honored my body and the season she was in, nothing fell apart.

So that's what this book is about. It's about honoring our bodies, pursuing our career dreams, and being proud of the kind of mothers we are. It's about creating space for what matters. It's about experimenting with small things we can try every day to *do less in order to have more.*

How to Use This Book

I'm not asking you to reinvent your entire life. Throughout this book, I'll simply suggest a new way to see something or a slightly different way to do something (or not do something) so that you can be your own scientist and see what happens.

Part I of this book will give you a new framework for looking at the world and your life that sets you up for doing less. Then Part II has 14 experiments for trying out specific, small ways of doing less in your daily life. It works really well as a two-week plan, but of course you can do it however floats your boat!

You can try out doing less as a solo experiment or gather some friends together to put it into practice as a group. I've found that the quickest way for me to implement a new belief system or behavior is to do it with support. So if it were me, I'd go the girlfriend route! (I made a guide for you to gather your women and do the experiments together at kate northrup.com/gifts.)

I've had many people raise their eyebrows in doubt when I start talking about doing less as a way to have more. (Although, really, the point is to *experience* more because this isn't really about *stuff*.) So if you're experiencing some healthy skepticism at this point, you're not alone, and the next chapter includes a ton of data on why doing less actually gets us better results, which should give your analytical brain something to chew on and be satisfied with.

I want to ask you to simply try doing less with me.

Most of us were only offered one model of success. It looked like this: pushing, working harder and harder, putting in more hours, putting in more effort, focusing on achievement above all else, the accumulation of status and material wealth, and being productive as a way of showing our worth.

Our society has a lot of rewards available for living that way. First of all, everyone around you respects you when you're busy. There's a certain feeling of wearing a badge of honor when we have sooooo much on our plates and we're crazy busy.

But this way of living has fallout too: *Always being distracted with your kids and having them long for your real and true presence. Feeling disconnected from your partner because you can't remember the last time you simply sat with each other and really listened to what was going on without having to rush off to another event or without checking your phone at the same time. Experiencing a sense of profound dissatisfaction and asking, "Is this really it?"*

I'm only asking you to try doing less as an experiment, because I bet you've never tried it before and therefore you have no evidence that it won't work.

Most of us have only tried the do-more way. We know the kind of results it gets us.

I never tried doing less until my body and baby essentially forced me to. I discovered that it works—at least for me and the few thousand women I've shared this with—by accident.

Now that I've been doing it on purpose for a couple of years, I can report that it works! *Really* well. My company is just about to close out our first-ever seven-figure year, and while I would have assumed the only way to create a business of that size would have been to work my butt off, I'm happy to report that I worked on average 20 to 25 hours a week this year and felt surprising ease and support around it.

What if you found out what happens when you do less on purpose? What I'm proposing is that if we work in sync with the cycles going on within us and around us, we'll find that we can do less, yet net more. And that we can feel more satisfaction, ease, and harmony as we do it.

There is a cosmic flow pulsing through us and around us at all times. This book is about tapping into that flow, steering our boat downstream, and letting life lead the way.

Let me be clear on one thing: This is not a "Look what I've done, you can do it too!" kind of book. This is a "Hey! I'm learning how to do this thing that I think is really important. Do you want to learn with me?" kind of book.

I invite us both to think critically about how it's been and how it could be. If we're both willing to think about it all differently, we'll be part of creating a new reality for our children (biological and otherwise) and ourselves.

There's no hierarchy here. We're in this together, shoulder to shoulder. Sister to sister.

We need to revolutionize the way we work. It's no longer acceptable to work as though we don't have bodies, as though we are not of nature.

This book is written for anyone who identifies as a woman who has the dual vocation of being a nurturer and having a career. I've used my own experience in motherhood as the lens to address ways we can change the way we work so that it actually works for, instead of against, our bodies, ourselves, humankind, and the planet. But please know that if you're not a mother in the traditional sense, the experiments and perspectives in this book absolutely apply to you and will help you if you implement them.

So when I say *mother*, feel free to replace that word with *nurturer* and apply the examples I use to your own life in a way that makes sense for your identity and lived experience.

There's nothing particularly easy about being a working mother. Or a stay-at-home mom. Or some combination of the two. Or a woman who takes care of other people and is also trying to make a living while taking care of herself. But there are some key things we can do to make it easier.

Adrienne Maree Brown says in her book *Emergent Strategy* that ease is sustainable. She reminds us that birds coast when they can.

That's what this book is about: finding as much ease as possible even as we do the things that aren't all that easy. It's about finding the places to coast when you can. It's about living and working in ways that make you resilient for the long haul. It's about sustainability, which to me means living and working in ways that will allow us, the beings around us, and the planet to thrive indefinitely.

We don't ask a flower to blossom all year long. We understand that she has seasons and cycles.

If we are to expect a shift in our culture where the feminine is honored and where the systems shift to support life, we must start by honoring the feminine in our own bodies. Only then will a shift ripple out.

So it starts with us.

Let's begin.

the
do less
philosophy

Before you dive head on into implementing doing less in your life, it's important to lay a foundation for why and how it can actually work for you as a life practice—even if it's only for the next two weeks! If you're reading this book, you're likely looking for an antidote to our *doing*-obsessed culture. Which means the belief system you were raised with was likely focused on doing more as the path to significance, success, worthiness, and wholeness.

First, I'm going to give you evidence of how doing less actually allows you to have more of what you really want. Part I includes data, examples from around the globe, and an invitation to look at your body, the planet, and your schedule in an entirely new way that will revolutionize the way you approach nearly everything.

You're going to learn how doing less is not a ticket to slacker-dom, as you might assume, but instead is an invitation to be more of your most fabulous self, which leaves you and the whole world better off than the burned-out, constantly-doing version of you. What you're about to experience has the potential to change your perspective on and experience of life forever; it did for me, which is why I wrote this book for you. Everything you've ever been taught about what it takes to create success and a life worth living is about to be questioned and quite possibly dismantled.

Ready? Let's go.

1

the
global evidence for
doing less

You bothered to open this book and start reading it, which to me says that you already believe, or at least suspect, that there might be something to this whole idea of doing less. From my own lived experience and the reports of the thousands of women I've worked with, I know down to my bone marrow how profoundly it can impact a life and make it more meaningful.

But data is good too, right? Something to feed the left hemispheres of our brains to satisfy their analytical appetites?

So I went on a little hunt with my friend, editor, and research assistant Julia Nickles. What we found was a boatload of evidence to support the idea that doing less actually results in having more in the realms of health, productivity, peace of mind, fulfillment, and happiness! Yay for data that tells us to do less.

The Data on Doing Less

But before we get to the data that tells us all the great results people around the world are getting from doing less, let's first talk about the evidence for why doing more isn't as good for us as we've all been conditioned to believe. Our health, our productivity, our creativity, and even our mental and emotional well-being have all suffered as a result.

In a research review published in *The Lancet* involving more than 600,000 men and women, it was found that a 55-hour workweek led to a 33 percent increase in stroke plus a 13 percent risk of coronary heart disease.[1] Another study found that working 49 hours a week was associated with poor mental health, especially in women. (The average person working full-time in the USA works 47 hours a week, and 4 out of 10 people work 50 or more hours per week.)[2]

These results are not surprising when you think about it. So many women are leaning out because the old model of putting in more hours and more effort literally makes us sick and less resilient mentally. Also, stress, like that caused from working longer hours, shrinks our gray matter (brain mass) in the area related to self-control.[3]

As Dr. Travis Bradberry, co-author of *Emotional Intelligence 2.0,* wrote: "Experiencing stress actually makes it more difficult to deal with future stress because it diminishes your ability to take control of the situation, manage your stress and keep things from getting out of control. A vicious cycle if there ever was one."

So how much should we actually be working? When does the law of diminishing returns set in?

In research reported by the *Harvard Business Review*, it was stated that very few people could be in a state of high concentration on things that really move the needle forward, like writing about new ideas, for more than four or five hours a day total. This held true even among extremely high performers, including athletes, novelists, and musicians. And, honestly, spending four to five hours a day on high-leverage activities like that is *impressive;* it's two hours more a day than average executives and managers devote to building their skills.[4]

David Rock, author of *Your Brain at Work*, found that we're truly focused on our work a mere six hours per week and that the average person focuses the best early in the morning or late at night, which our standard workday is totally not supportive of. The average worker in an office gets interrupted every 3 to 10 minutes, and it could take from 5 to 25 minutes to get refocused on what you were doing before.[5]

Interestingly, though, we've evolved from a survival standpoint to interrupt ourselves. Forty-four percent of our interruptions are self-inflicted because our brains want to make sure that we're aware of potential harm in our environment. Therefore, focus takes training. It's more about what you say no to than what you say yes to. (More on that later in the book.)

Mothers are celebrated for multitasking, and that ability is praised in a lot of workplaces too. In environments addicted to the hustle, doing more is worn like a badge of honor. But the real truth about trying to do multiple things at the same time is that it drops our IQ and makes us miss important information and make mistakes more often.[6]

In addition to logging a 40-plus-hour workweek without any evidence of its effectiveness, we've also been programmed to work for hours on end without any breaks. But the evidence shows that this "suck it up and put your head down" behavior isn't doing us any favors either.

A study reported in *Business Insider* found that people who took regular breaks were wildly more productive than those who kept their butt in their chair for hours on end without pausing to refresh.[7] The ideal ratio was approximately one 15-minute break to every hour of work—or, more specifically, 52 minutes of work and an average of 17 minutes of rest. These regular breaks allowed people to stay 100 percent focused on a specific activity without distracting themselves with social media, texts, or anything else. Most of us push through fatigue, and our work after the push decreases in quality, as does our mental state. This study suggests that if we take a real break at the first wave of fatigue—and go for a walk, meditate, have a snack, do some yoga, fold some laundry, or chat with a friend—we'll be way more productive than if we push through.

If we're only truly focused on our work for a total of six hours a week and the office environment breeds interruptions that make us ineffective, it makes sense that some forward-thinking leaders around the world are waking up to the fact that sitting at a desk for just over nine hours a day, which is the average amount that people in the U.S. work, is actually not a great use of our time.

Doing Less Around the Globe

Let's take a little tour around the globe to find out how other countries are organizing themselves, given the truth of the fact that our typical 40-plus-hour workweek isn't serving our health or our productivity.

First we head to Sweden, where they're moving toward a national standard of a six-hour workday for the well-being of workers. (Imagine considering the well-being of human beings as one of your factors of success!) They've realized that working more does not necessarily get better results since it's virtually impossible to stay focused for eight hours anyway. What companies like the Stockholm-based app development company Filimundus are finding is that if you stay off social media and minimize distractions and meetings during your workday, the reduction in hours hasn't reduced productivity one bit. Plus, since staff are happier, there are fewer office conflicts, which saves a ton of time and energy, and people are able to exercise, be with their families, and pursue passions outside of work too![8]

When we pop over to the UK, we meet Dr. John Ashton, who has declared that the entire nation should go down to a four-day workweek. He claims it will make people healthier by reducing blood pressure and mental illness as well as balance a "maldistribution of work" in which some people work way too much and some people are unemployed.[9] Interesting stuff, especially when you begin to consider economics on a national and global scale.

Right here in the U.S., the software company Basecamp (formerly known as 37signals) takes a nod from Mother Nature, acknowledging that though software may not be a seasonal business, humans remain affected by seasons and cycles. (Way to go, CEO Jason Fried! You and I speak the same language.) From May through October, the entire company has a four-day workweek of 32 hours in total—not mashing the usual 40-plus-hour week into four days.

In a 2012 op-ed for *The New York Times*, Fried said he found that better work gets done in a four-day rather than five-day workweek because the compressed schedule forces you to focus on what's important. The company also allowed everyone to work on whatever they wanted for the month of June, and Fried reported that it resulted in the biggest burst of creativity that the company has ever seen.[10]

Working less + freedom = creativity + productivity. Boom.

In 2018, a New Zealand firm that manages trusts, wills, and estates, Perpetual Guardian, implemented a four-day workweek while still paying its employees for five days. They found that productivity increased and their employees' job performance didn't change at all. The company is looking to make this change permanent given its success.[11]

Anna Coote, the head of social policy at New Economics, has even gone so far as to recommend a 21-hour workweek. (I love a bold lady!) What survey after survey has proven is that workers who feel in control of their workflow and their own time (meaning less of it is taken up by work so they can do more of the things they want to do outside of work) are actually way more productive and creative than workers who feel like they're not getting paid enough to work as hard as they do. The article in *The New Yorker* that reviews Coote's recommendation follows up with:

> While feeling in control and working fewer hours may seem like distinct issues, they are fundamentally connected. When we own more of our time, we feel like we're in charge of our lives and our schedules, which makes us happier and, ultimately, better at what we do. Our health and happiness also increases in the course of our lifetimes and, with it, our value to the workplace and to society as a whole. Additionally, we may finally recover from chronic sleep deprivation, which is one of the greatest health hazards currently facing the average employee. Sleep quality, in turn, translates to better cognition, clearer thinking, and increased productivity. Instead of the usual vicious circle, we get a virtuous one.[12]

Amen. Amen. Amen.

There's even support for a *three*-day workweek. Back in Gothenburg, Sweden, Toyota centers switched to a three-day workweek in 2003 and report happier staff, lower turnover rate, and an increase in profits as a result.[13] Beyond the benefits of happier, healthier workers and more productivity, thought leaders like Carlos Slim, Mexico's richest man, says that a three-day workweek would allow more jobs for younger people and the benefit of older workers staying in the workforce longer so that the company could be blessed with their wisdom and expertise.[14]

So there you have it. A lot of great research suggesting that doing less and taking lots of breaks is not only good for you but also for productivity, profitability, and humanity in general.

As we dive deeper together, you're going to learn about creative cycles and seasons, as well as how our brains are wired for different types of activities depending on what time of the month or year it is.

When you combine honoring your beautifully cyclical, nonlinear working nature with the evidence I just shared with you about how we need a new approach to our workday and workweek to support our well-being and the well-being of the organizations we work within, you'll see that doing less really does, in fact, net more.

2

your worth,
your cycles,
and momentum

One of the biggest crises of identity faced by women who've had flourishing careers before starting our families—including those I've worked with and those I've been friends with, as well as myself—is that when we have kids, we suddenly feel like we have nothing to show for our days. Whereas a day well spent might once have included landing a new deal, giving a great presentation, and having several pages' worth of a proposal completed at the end, now the pile of laundry is bigger, the same dish has been washed three times, and the house looks way worse than it did in the morning. Plus, we're way more tired at the end of the day than we used to be after having put in eight hours at the office.

Oh yeah, and there's no break in sight, because now it's time to make dinner, do the dishes, clean up the kitchen, get the kids in and out of the tub, chase them up and down the hall trying to get them in a diaper and wrangle them into pajamas, get them calm enough to read a story, and, finally, if it's a good night, have them pass out before 8:30 P.M. so we can have a few minutes to breathe (or space out on our phones) before crashing ourselves.

Theoretically, raising the next generation is the most important job in the world. So why do so many of us feel like the work we do with our families doesn't mean as much as the work we do that earns money?

The way our economy works, we earn money in exchange for doing something or offering something that someone else values. So where does that leave us as women and mothers?

It leaves us doing incredibly valuable work in a society that really doesn't value it.

Here's the deal: Our society values the traditional qualities of the masculine over the traditional qualities of the feminine. I'm not talking men versus women here. I'm talking about the two kinds of energy that we have within us, though most of us tend to lead more with one than the other.

Traditional qualities of the masculine:	Traditional qualities of the feminine:
• Productive	• Nurturing
• Linear	• Intuitive
• Analytical	• Cyclical
• Aggressive	• Looks for win/win scenarios
• Logical	
• Competitive	• Emotional
• Results-oriented	• Process-oriented
• Win/lose mentality	• "Being" over "doing"
• "Doing" over "being"	• Flow
• Structure	• Inward
• Outward	• Receptive
• Individualism	• Community
• "Me"	• "We"

As a woman, do you ever feel like the world just isn't designed to support who you are at your core? That in order to succeed you have to shut down your intuition, your emotions, and other parts of yourself and be more like a man?

That's because the world we live in is set up to support the masculine. It's not designed to support the feminine.

Something I learned from my friend Alisa Vitti, founder of FloLiving.com and author of *WomanCode,* is that both men and women are cyclical. However, women cycle on a 28-day rotation while men cycle on a 24-hour rotation. Men go through all of the phases in a day, and women go through them in a month. And because we live in a patriarchy that celebrates the masculine over the feminine, our whole world is set up to support a 24-hour cycle, not a 28-day cycle.

We're supposed to show up at the same time every day and put in as much or more effort and intensity than we put in yesterday. The idea is to grow no matter what the cost to others, our bodies, our psyches, or our families. But innately, the way the world is set up doesn't reflect the way that women's bodies are wired.

During our reproductive years, we cycle on a roughly 28-day rotation with four distinct phases. Each phase has its own unique gifts and opportunities if we pay attention to them. And each phase literally and metaphorically holds critical ingredients to complete a full cycle of creation.

Let me walk you through what I'm talking about because if you're anything like me, you had NO IDEA that your body was innately wired with so much power and wisdom. Sex ed basically covers how not to get pregnant. They missed the whole part about how ingenious our bodies are and how within them they hold the blueprint for creation.

I cannot believe I didn't realize the total powerhouse within me that is the menstrual cycle until I was 34 years old and already a mother—especially given that I grew up with a mother who was teaching this stuff and one of the biggest global champions for it. But it just shows you how loud the messages are within our culture that talking about the wisdom of the female body is weird or that periods are gross and should just be dealt with in private, not talked about, and ideally medicated away.

It took me having a profoundly fallow creative period for me to even be open to what my inner rhythms might have to do with my outer world. It took me actually bringing life into this world to suddenly realize how wise and powerful my body really is! There's nothing like holding a beautiful human baby in your arms to make you realize that your body is really a freaking miracle.

Whether you have a biological child or not, and no matter what organs you still have in your body and how they are or aren't functioning, you have this very same energetic blueprint within you. Later on I'll get into how to track your cycle and use it even if you're not cycling because you're past menopause, are pregnant, are nursing, have had a hysterectomy, or some other reason. The miracle of working with your cycles is available for all women (and even men), so keep reading and I promise you'll see how it applies to you as this all unfolds. Everyone gets to play.

The Menstrual Cycle

Okay, let's dive into the menstrual cycle first, and then we'll get to how to use this cycle in your life to do less and have more.

Now, I won't say which phase is the first, second, or third, etc., because it's a cycle and it's nonlinear. I'll just start with talking about the follicular phase because it's about new beginnings.

The follicular phase biologically is when the egg-producing follicles in your ovaries begin to mature and the ovary gets ready to release an egg. This happens after you bleed during the menstrual phase of your period. The lining of your uterus begins to build up, ready to welcome a possible pregnancy. Energetically, it's when you're the most primed to plan, to plant seeds of creation and desire, to brainstorm, and to initiate new projects.

After the follicular phase comes the ovulation phase, when your physical body is most fertile and you're also energetically and creatively the most fertile. Within your body, an ovary has released an egg and it's ready and available to be fertilized at this time. You release pheromones at this time, chemicals that have been proven to make you more attractive to the opposite sex (and perhaps the same sex too).[1] Based on what's going on hormonally in your body at this time, you'll actually be the most articulate and magnetic during this phase.

Energetically, the ovulation phase is the perfect time to get out there and get the word out about what you're working on. It's a great time for making sales calls, doing presentations, and pitching your ideas. Be open to collaborations and working with others because, energetically, you're the most fertile. You'll also be the most receptive and magnetic at this time, and you can really take advantage of that by tapping into your "Egg Wisdom." (This is a concept that I learned from my mom, Christiane Northrup, M.D., and that I'll be covering in more depth in this book.)

The luteal phase starts when you ovulate and ends when you menstruate. While all the phases are powerful, this is one of the most misunderstood and overlooked for the power it holds. The luteal phase marks the time in your cycle when your energy begins to turn inward. The follicular and ovulation phases are outward times and the luteal and menstrual phases are inward times. (More on this inward versus outward conversation in a moment.)

During the luteal phase, the corpus luteum, which is what's left of the ovarian follicle that was housing the egg that was released at ovulation, produces progesterone. This hormone turns the endometrium, or uterine lining, into a soft bed to welcome a fertilized egg. (This hormone is also responsible for helping us feel calm and serene.) The luteal phase lasts 12 to 14 days in most women. So the luteal phase is actually brilliantly designed by the Goddess herself to be a little longer than the other phases of your cycle. Why?

During the luteal phase, you're energetically poised to complete projects. To dot your i's and cross your t's. To bring it on home. So this is the perfect time to be wrapping up the project that you initiated during the follicular phase. Your brain chemistry is supporting focus and the ability to finish things. You may not feel like going out to every networking event or party during this phase, but it's a great time to hunker down, wrap things up, and begin to slow down before the next phase of the cycle.

If you're anything like me, a great starter but not typically that into finishing things, then tracking your cycle and really honoring your luteal phase is going to make quantum shifts in your ability to have more by doing less. (More on how tracking your cycle can help you do less in Experiment #1.)

Finally, we have the menstrual phase of your whole cycle. This is the time when you bleed. It can be a little confusing because we call the whole 28 day-ish shebang the menstrual cycle but then one of the phases is also called the menstrual cycle. So you could also call this phase the bleed, if you want to make sure you're crystal clear on what's going on here.

If, during a cycle, the egg your body released has not been fertilized, then during this phase your body releases the uterine lining that's been building up ever since the follicular phase. The corpus luteum stops producing progesterone, which signals the uterine lining to release and prepare for the next round.

Energetically, the time when you bleed is the ideal time for rest and reflection. Your brain is the most wired for connectivity between the left and right hemispheres right now, which makes you super smart and able to integrate logical and intuitive information with remarkable clarity. Your physical energy will likely be the lowest during this time, so it's a great time to take a day off, minimize social engagements, do super gentle movement (if any), and just rest.

This is also a great time to evaluate what's working and what's not working in your life. In the book *Wild Power* by Alexandra Pope and Sjaine Hugo Wurlitzer, they talk about bringing a question or quandary to your menstrual phase and "bleeding on it" as opposed to thinking on it. This is such a powerful way to do less! Saving your evaluation for when your brain is the most primed for this kind of activity and to have the most clarity the quickest is one of the best ways I can think of to save time by not obsessing and overthinking things.

Again, we're not supported in our daily lives to turn our energy inward because that's a more feminine energy approach, and our cultural beliefs and structures are set up to support constant outward energy. But those who are introverted, who have studied Eastern philosophy, or who really honor the half of their cycle that includes the luteal and menstrual phases know very intimately how being outward all the time can completely fry your circuits and lead to burnout.

The Universe is a whole bucket of duality. Light and dark. Stillness and movement. Wet and dry. Quiet and loud. Fast and slow. Inward and outward. Without one quality or energy, the other one couldn't exist, and both are critical to the whole.

So, if we force ourselves to stay in the outward energy that's supported by the follicular and ovulation portions of our cycle and ignore the luteal and menstrual phases, we're missing out on not only half of the juicy experience of being a woman, but also a full half of our creative potential.

I'm a massive extrovert. I just get more and more wound up and happy, like a hummingbird, the more I spend time with people. Put me in a room of people I love, and I will happily buzz about for hours. When I leave, I'll feel more like myself, closer to God, and like all is well with the world. And I'll have no problem hopping right into the next social event.

So the turning inward and honoring the parts of the cycle that aren't about going out there and getting things done has been historically really challenging for me. In fact, I managed to pretty much ignore it until I got pregnant at 32 and my body put the brakes on big-time. She was like, "Okay, sister. You've been going strong out there cross-pollinating and making things happen for 32 years. Time to bring it in. Time to replenish. Time to rest. Time to stop doing and see who you are underneath all of that activity."

That's a question I encourage everyone to ask themselves, man or woman: *Who am I if I'm not doing anything? Who am I if I'm not producing? Who am I if I'm not in action?*

So many of us have been raised to believe that our worth is equal to our accomplishments. That we must earn our deserving of life and all things good through doing. But this couldn't possibly be true if we also believe, as I do, that our worth is inherent, that no person is born more or less worthy than another, that we are all children of God/Goddess and that we deserve to be here no matter how high we climb on the ladder of success.

In Bronnie Ware's book *The Top Five Regrets of the Dying*, based on her deep conversations with the dying as a palliative care worker, she doesn't reveal that most people regret not being more successful when they're on their deathbed. They don't regret not having achieved more. In fact, the top five regrets were:

- Wishing they'd had the courage to live a life more true to themselves rather than the life others expected of them.

- Wishing they hadn't worked so hard.

- Wishing they'd had the courage to express their feelings.

- Wishing they'd stayed in touch with their friends.

- Wishing they'd let themselves be happier.

Even now, having read these before, as I write them here they hit me like Aunty Em's house dropping out of the sky from a tornado right on top of the Wicked Witch of the East. Just my little stocking feet sticking out, shriveling up in realization that our programming is SO DEEP.

We are raised to believe that what matters most is:

- Living up to the expectations of our parents, our communities, and our society.

- Working really hard and as much as possible.

- Not being so emotional.

- Getting ahead.

- Achievement and that it will make us happy (though the more and more we rack up achievements, the more and more we know this one just isn't true, despite the fact that we keep doing it).

Yet the top regrets of the dying are in *exact opposition* to the core beliefs that most of us are raised with, probably not explicitly, but they're certainly the blood that runs through the veins of our educational system, organized sports, and pretty much every industry I'm aware of.

Now listen, on the other side of this is one of my favorite quotes, attributed to Albert Einstein: "Nothing happens until something moves."

And it's so true. If we're not working on something, we get a little lackadaisical and even, maybe, depressed. But we get our panties all in a wrinkle because we forget that the happiness comes from the *process* of progress and growth, not from the *result* of progress and growth.

I recently learned of a Montessori education practice in which a kid who paints a picture or produces something else tangible isn't congratulated on how great the result is. Instead, they ask the kid what the process was like. What colors did you use to create your picture? What did it feel like to hold the brush? What were you thinking about while you made it? What was it like to paint this picture?

What would we be like as adults if all of our parents, teachers, and caregivers, instead of handing us a gold star or a medal for an A or being first in line or drawing the most lifelike still life, had asked us what it was like to be in the process of learning our spelling words or running the race or putting our pencil to paper while looking at a beautiful flower arrangement?

We wouldn't be so confused about what matters, that's what.

It's not too late. As long as we have a pulse, it's never too late. While the best time to start would have been yesterday, the second best is always today. (Actually, I believe in reincarnation, so I don't even think it's too late after we die. I'm pretty sure we always get another chance, so we can just chill the F out.)

Okay, so here we are wondering who we are if our worth is not solely based on our accomplishments. And as women, we're waking up to the idea that there's some untapped wisdom in our bodies' natural way that can actually help us have more by doing less.

Cyclical Living for All of Us (Menstruating or Not)

I promised I would tell you why you're not left out if you're not cycling for whatever reason, so now I will. (I'm a woman of my word, after all.) We all get to play when it comes to cycles!

What's so ingenious and infinitely cool about the cyclical nature of women is that it mirrors the cycles of the moon exactly. And on a macro scale, it also mimics the four seasons. So, whether you have your own personal cycle or not, the moon is always there as a guide and all you have to do is get yourself a lunar calendar or do a quick Google search to find out what phase the moon is in and start there. The new moon, or dark of the moon, is the same energy as the bleeding time of a menstrual cycle.

When I was living as part of the crew of a schooner in college with very little artificial light, at sea for two weeks at a time without seeing land, all of the women on the ship started cycling with the new moon, meaning we would start bleeding the very same day the moon was completely invisible in the night sky.

This isn't unusual. Women tend to cycle with the new moon when their bodies aren't being impacted by artificial light and they also tend to cycle together when living in community. Isn't that amazing?

21

Your Cycle and the Moon

If your period doesn't come on the new moon, there's nothing wrong with you. We don't live in total communion with Mother Nature (or at least most of us don't), so there's no reason to beat yourself up for when you start your cycle. Cycling at different times of the lunar cycle simply gives you a different experience of your cycle, perhaps gentler or perhaps more intense.

My recommendation is to simply track your experience of your cycle in relation to the moon if this is of interest to you. (I've included the Daily Energy Tracker that I created for my Origin® Planner in Appendix A, which includes a spot for you to record both the day of your cycle and the phase of the moon.)

You may find that you have more energy during the menstrual phase of your cycle if you bleed with the full moon or that your intuition is on superdrive. And you can also play around with it. I've found that if I set the intention to begin to cycle with the new moon, over the course of a couple of months my cycle usually shifts and before I know it, I start to bleed the day the moon is dark. Super, super cool.

Given that the new moon is a similar energy to the menstrual phase of the body's cycle, this is a great time for rest and reflection. If you like to do rituals, it's also a great time to set intentions for what you'd like to manifest over the next lunar cycle before the moon is new again. I'm all about efficiency, so I like to keep my rituals super-duper simple; usually, I just light a candle and write a list of new moon desires in a journal. It takes about five minutes. But you can certainly go nuts and get out your crystals and incense and Goddess cards and ritual garb. Totally up to you.

Waxing

The waxing moon is the next phase, when the moon is getting bigger. (Well, in reality, the moon moves at an angle to the sun, so that as more sunlight is being reflected off of it we can see it more and more as each day passes.) This is a similar energy to the follicular phase of your cycle, so it's a great time for brainstorming, planning, and initiating projects.

Full

Next up is the full moon, which technically only lasts one day, but the few days before and after are part of the phase. The energy around this time is the same as the ovulation phase of the menstrual cycle. It's about peak receptivity, peak fertility, and peak visibility. This can be a really great time to be out, get the word out about what you're working on, strike up deals, pitch your ideas, and all other things that get you and your stuff out there.

The Energy of the Full Moon

The full moon can have an incredibly intense energy. Start tracking the moon and taking some notes on the full moon around how you feel and how your kids are acting. I find that around the full moon, Penelope tends to not sleep as well and her emotions are often more volatile. I love knowing that there's a cosmic factor in this because it makes me feel more relaxed as her mother and more supportive of her experience. Rather than thinking there's something wrong with her or that I'm doing something wrong or that I need to fix something, I can simply surrender into experiencing the intensity of the full moon energy with her. As a mom, the more reasons I have to not feel like I'm doing something wrong and simply be with my kids, the better!

After the moon is full, it begins to decrease in visibility as it continues its journey around the earth and gets farther away from the sun. This phase is called the waning moon, and it has the same energy as the luteal phase of the menstrual cycle. This is a great time to begin to slow things down, wrap things up, turn your energy inward, and do anything that needs to be done to finish up whatever project or manifestation you were working on during this particular lunar cycle.

Then we're back at the new moon again and everything starts over.

The Power of Cyclical Living

Here's what's so awesome about living cyclically: it really helps quell the feeling of running out of time.

A few years back I was in Costa Rica with my family, celebrating my dad's 65th birthday. We were on one of those group outdoor adventure trips, so every night we ended up having dinner with other families and getting to know them.

One night I was chatting with another woman on the trip at a long teak table on a huge, canopied outdoor deck with howler monkeys calling in the distance, and somehow we got on the topic of synesthesia. The synesthesia I'd heard of is a phenomenon where a small portion of the population either tastes shapes or colors. So when they think of a shape or a color they have a certain taste in their mouths that's associated with it. The definition is a sensory experience where you associate a specific sensation with something else. Some people see sounds, associate numbers with certain colors, or have all kinds of novel ways of perceiving the sensory world.[2]

As we got to chatting, though, this woman told me that that wasn't the only kind of synesthesia there is.

"Point to the month of May," she said to me.

It was an odd direction to give me, but I knew exactly what she meant.

I pointed to the bottom left-hand portion of an imaginary circle in front of my face, about where 8 P.M. would be if that circle were a clock.

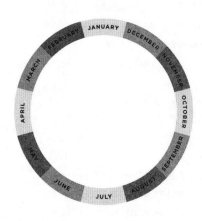

MY VISUALIZATION OF THE YEAR

"That's synesthesia too," she said. "You can see time, but not everyone can."

We got to talking, and I realized that I had always seen time visually in my mind's eye and that it was a circle was not typical. In fact, when I looked it up I found out only an estimated 4 percent of the population has synesthesia of any kind, which is basically a jumbling of the senses. The type of synesthesia where people "see time" in this way is known as "sequence-space synesthesia." Although it is less well known as the kind where you taste numbers or associate colors with shapes, it is actually way more common! People who have this see ordinal sequences like numbers, months, or the letters of the alphabet as occupying a specific spatial location in their mind's eye.[3]

A few years later, I was on the phone with my sister sitting at my gate at JFK Airport, waiting to board my connection flight home to Portland, Maine. I was just starting to do more research about the power of cycles in our bodies and in the cosmos and seeing the connections between these two things and the way we create things like books, courses, products, dinner parties, or any other creative endeavor we pursue.

We got on the topic of calendar synesthesia, as she was part of that conversation years before in Costa Rica. We were talking about how cool it is that I've always seen the calendar as a circle so time has always been cyclical to me, regardless of the fact that I've always lived in a world that tells me it's linear.

"Yeah," my brilliant sister said, "and when you look at a day as a circle it's so relaxing because as the day goes on you're always moving back toward the beginning of a new day instead of running out of time in the day you're currently in."

Whoa! Mind. Blown.

I'd never applied my mind's wacky conception of cyclical annual time to a 24-hour period. But on the next flight, I went crazy drawing circles all over my notebook using the bottom of my little plastic beverage service cup as a template. I divided it into 24 separate little slices of time pie and played with all the ways that the 24 hours of a day could also be overlaid with the cycles of the moon, the menstrual cycle, and even the four seasons.

Anyone looking at me would have thought I was Rain Man or something. My enthusiasm radiated off my body and I just kept drawing circle after circle after circle. Finally, I landed upon what I now call the Daily Renewable Planner, which is a way to see a day as a circle rather than a linear block of hours. (See Appendix B.)

When I shared this concept with the women in Origin, my membership program for entrepreneurial women who want to cut through their overwhelm and have more by doing less, they were similarly as blown away as I was by how simply looking at time as a circle instead of a line made their bodies instantly relax and made them feel suddenly like there was enough time.

Our bodies already know that everything is a circle, that we're coming back here again, that there's no such thing as running out of time, that the Universe is infinitely abundant, and that everything is predictably rhythmic. But we've forgotten this truth for so very long, and it's sent us running the "race to nowhere," as described by Dr. Shefali Tsabary, best-selling author of *The Awakened Family* among others.

When we begin to perceive our bodies, our energy, and time as cyclical instead of linear, we not only feel relaxed on a cellular level in a way most of us have never experienced, we also begin to pick up momentum without having to struggle.

Alisa Vitti gave me a great analogy for this. Imagine you have a hockey puck and a bicycle tire on a flat surface like a really big area of concrete. You give the hockey puck a push, and it goes for a while but eventually stops. You give the bicycle tire a push, and it keeps rolling for as long as it can stay upright and not run into an obstacle. In many cases, it actually gains speed as it goes.

The hockey puck is flat, but the tire is a circle. The flat one stops. The circular one keeps going.

This is the power of cyclical momentum.

When we honor the distinct and uniquely useful phases of our bodies, the moon, and our creativity, we get further, faster, without having to push as hard. It's like having spent your whole life furiously paddling against a really strong current and suddenly realizing that all you needed to do to cover more ground was turn your canoe downstream and use your paddle to steer every now and again.

The current of Mother Earth and the Universe is already going this way. We just need to join her.

It's so important to get that so much of our world, our bodies, and our very nature as women is cyclical, not linear. And now that we know that, in the next chapter I'm going to teach you how to practically apply a cyclical lens to your work and any project, really anything creative, that you're doing. When you start to see and organize your creativity and workflow as cyclical instead of linear, you'll shift from feeling like there's never enough time and you'll never get it all done to feeling like you're in flow with the creative forces that be. You'll find yourself having more than enough time and energy to do what you need to do, *and* you'll be way better at drawing a line between what needs to be done and what doesn't. It's a total game changer. Off we go!

3

the upward cycle
of success

When I started geeking out on the menstrual cycle and the way it's a microcosm of the seasons and mirrors the lunar cycle, I felt incredibly held. I could see that I was part of this grand design that had been going on all along without me even having to be conscious of it to benefit from it. There's so much about feminine energy and wisdom that keeps on trucking without our intellect needing to be on board. That's what's so ingenious about it.

Take, for example, growing a human being inside of you. I was acutely aware during my first pregnancy that I was doing NOTHING but that so much was happening. I was in deep awe and reverence of my body for the first time in my life. My body was growing a human and I didn't have to be conscious of it, make a to-do list, prioritize, learn a thing, or lift a finger. It was all happening based on the divine design of being a woman.

I remember giving a talk at the Reveal Retreat at Kripalu, while six months pregnant, and saying, "I could be growing an ear or a liver right now and I don't even have to think about it or even *know* about it!" I couldn't help but begin to look at what might happen, though, if I did tune in to the cycles and seasons all around me consciously as a lifestyle as opposed to just let them happen without me thinking about it.

I've long known that what we put our attention on grows. One of my favorite quotes of all time is: "What we appreciate appreciates." (I don't know who said it, but I love it.) So I hypothesized that if I paid attention to the cycles going on within me and around me and participated with them on purpose that I could get the same kind of results that Mother Nature gets: massive abundance, beauty, diversity, and life force. I could naturally have more by doing less.

At the time, my first baby girl was a little over a year old. I was still nursing, still working part-time, and we were still mega struggling when it came to sleep and her poor, red, itchy skin. When I gave a toast thanking our very nearest and dearest inner circle at Penelope's birthday party, I just burst into tears, saying that there's no way we would have made it without their help because it was just so freaking hard.

I needed to tap into something to hold me beyond our amazing community, though. I needed something bigger. So I started simply tracking my own menstrual cycle and writing down how I felt each day depending on what day of my cycle I was in and what phase I was in.

This act alone was illuminating for two reasons: I stopped being surprised by my period coming every month and finding myself out and about without a tampon like I was 13. Also, I began to notice the deeper intricacies of my experience of being a woman and, more important, I began to honor them.

As I became more intimate with my own cycle, I started to bring in the phases of the moon for an added flavor to see how my body and my energy levels and emotions really were affected by the moon. (The word *lunatic* is actually based on the meaning "affected by the moon." I was pretty sure I was a lunatic, but I wanted evidence.)

Then I started thinking about the four seasons as macrocosms for the four kinds of energy and phases of any creative endeavor. The world all started making a lot more sense to me.

Because I'm practical and like to see how new ideas and approaches actually create results in the world, I began to apply the same four energies of the menstrual cycle, the lunar cycle, and the seasons to our business. What came

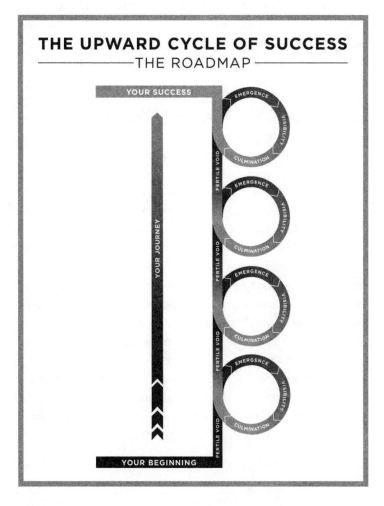

out of it is something I call the Upward Cycle of Success, which can be applied to any business as a whole but also to any individual project.

If human life is created based on these four phases and our planet is dictated by them, they're good enough for my business, I thought.

The reason it's the *Upward* Cycle of Success and not just the Cycle of Success is that you don't visit each phase just one time. In fact, you'll keep circling around all four phases until the project is complete or until this particular business is no longer in operation. But each time we revisit a certain phase, we've moved up the spiral so that we're visiting it at a higher level of consciousness and from a more evolved place than the last time.

It's kind of like when you're dealing with your mother issues in therapy. You've been to therapy before but more stuff is coming up, so you figure it's time to go back. And there you are getting all teary about the very same stuff you were getting choked up about 15 years before. *I thought I dealt with this already!* you think. Well, you did. But it's back again. Because life is a cycle, and you're revisiting it. But it's not the same as last time because you've had more life experience. You've done some healing in the meantime. You've grown more compassionate for yourself and your mother. Perhaps you've become a mother yourself. So now you may very well be crying about the same event or behavior from your childhood, but it's from a totally different level of consciousness and a higher level of personal evolution. Same issue. New perspective. Upward cycle.

When I released the concept of the Upward Cycle of Success to the world in May 2017, so many women reported back that they felt such a deep sense of relief and now had the framework they could use to truly create the career they desired within. They'd tried the other way of pushing and hustling and trying to find more hours in the day and self-sacrificing and expending every last drop of energy they had, and then some. But it wasn't working.

Either they'd quit pursuing their dreams outside motherhood, thinking they just couldn't have the career they desired and be present with their families at the same time, or they were totally burned out and hanging on by a thread. Or they'd suffered health consequences. Or they were stuck and depressed, unable to get any forward momentum.

But here was a framework that built in rest *on purpose*, not as a default. As one woman in our Origin community says, this way of being makes self-care part of our *rhythm* as opposed to a *reward*.

These women felt for the first time that this was a way they could imagine working for years to come without burnout, without their families suffering, without their health going into the toilet, and without feeling frazzled all the time.

This was a framework grounded in the truth of who we are as women, the truth of where humans came from, the truth of how our bodies were designed to create in the first place.

Fertile Void

I like to start my explanation of the Upward Cycle of Success with the Fertile Void because it's the most misunderstood, judged, avoided, and ignored phase of creation.

I found myself in a Fertile Void of sorts after my first book came out in 2013. I didn't have my next big idea. I didn't have it in me to write another book. I felt pretty dried up when it came to talking about money. I'd put everything I had to say about it in the book, and I didn't have anything new to add.

I wish I'd had the framework that I'm sharing with you right now at that time, because, as so many of us do, instead of recognizing that I was in a creative fallow period that's totally natural and even necessary for the next phase of creation to begin, I just thought there was something wrong with me.

In nature, the winter comes every year. I live in Maine, where the seasons are super pronounced and you really can't miss winter. The leaves fall off the deciduous trees. The branches are bare, and the trees look dead basically from December through late March. The ground is frozen. Nothing grows. The animals are hibernating, aside from some brazen squirrels running around on warmer days and the crows that never seem to stop cawing, no matter how freezing it is outside. It's gray, and doing anything outside in the world feels hard (because it is).

But, despite wishing it would come sooner, we never worry that spring isn't going to come next. We trust that eventually the temperatures will increase, the snow will melt (even if it doesn't happen until April), the animals will reappear, the leaves will begin to bud, and the crocuses will tenaciously push their way through the frozen earth, sometimes next to a little pile of snow, signaling to us that, yes, in fact, it's time for a new beginning.

The earth needs this time of rest. Even if you live somewhere closer to the equator, where the seasons aren't quite so pronounced, you'll notice signs of Mother Earth taking a break for a few months out of the year. The soil needs a break to refertilize. Animals need to take a long snooze. Trees and other plants turn inward for some downtime.

Interestingly enough, the seasons affect us humans too, beyond the kind of clothing we wear. The parts of our brain related to attention and concentration are the least active during the shorter days of the year in the winter months and the most active during the summer months.[1] It's not just the bears who need a break!

So the Fertile Void is our own creative winter. During the period from October 2013 until November 2016, I didn't have a lot of creative juice to make anything new. I kept working on projects that were already in motion, and I certainly put some new things out into the world. From the outside, you may not have known that I was in a Fertile Void because our business kept running and we kept doing things.

Inside, however, I knew that I wasn't tapped into my creative source in the way I wanted to be. I was lying fallow. I wish it hadn't taken three years to get the next big idea. I wish I'd only needed a month or two to be in the Fertile Void, but the thing about the Upward Cycle of Success is that each phase just takes as long as it takes. Just like you don't want to pull the baby out until it's full term if you can help it, you want to let the ideas cook as long as they need to so that they can really thrive in the outside world.

During the Fertile Void of a business or project, you might also feel anxious that you're not inspired enough or that you aren't doing enough. Don't worry, that's just the cultural brainwashing that raised us to believe that our worth is equal to our achievements and that if we're not doing anything, we're essentially worthless. This is a lie, however, and the sooner we become conscious of the lies we tell ourselves about who we really are, the sooner we get to actually be who we really are.

The Fertile Void is here to teach us that we are more than what we do, that there is tremendous value in rest, and that rest is even productive. Later on in the book, I'll tell you more about the incredible value of sleep and other forms of rest.

Emergence

The next phase of creation is Emergence, and it has the same energy as the follicular phase of your menstrual cycle, the waxing moon, and springtime. This is when your idea begins to take shape.

Let's say you're putting together a workshop. During the Fertile Void phase, you might have been doing some research or, even more passively, just noodling on ideas at random times like in the grocery line or the shower. But now things are getting more concrete.

This would be the part where you start to jot down notes and ideas. You might write an outline of the workshop and get clear on what you want participants to take away from it. This is when you'd be working on the title of the workshop, figuring out what the content will be, and planning out a timeline for when you want to have it ready to go, when you want to start spreading the word, and when it will be delivered.

Emergence is when a project moves from theoretical into concrete. And then it's time to put it out into the world.

Visibility

After Emergence comes Visibility. This is when it's time for your project to start making its way into the public eye. It's the same energy as ovulation, the full moon, and the peak of summertime. This is the time when you press publish, launch, and ship. In the life cycle of a workshop, Visibility would start when you open registration for your workshop, and then it would peak as you're actually teaching the workshop live.

Some activities to focus on during Visibility would be pitching investors or influencers on supporting your project, doing launch events like trade shows, making media appearances, using social media to gain traction, letting your existing audience know what's coming, making offers, and anything else you can think of to get the word out about your project. The flip side of putting yourself out there during Visibility is receptivity. Just like during ovulation, this is the time when our idea is at its peak magnetism. This is really a time to focus on your manifesting abilities and attraction just as much as, if not more than, getting out there and making things happen.

We'll talk more about this in the next chapter on Egg Wisdom, but for now let's simply remember that we don't have to work our asses off and hustle 24/7 in order to manifest every single thing we want to happen. There's a whole Universe out there available to support us, but in order for it to be able to do that we have to be aware that it's there and be willing to ask for and receive its support.

In a world where we've been taught that our worth is equal to how much we personally can achieve, it can be hard to simply relax and receive, because on some level we feel like we're less worthy if things come easily or we get help.

But remember Bronnie Ware and the five regrets of the dying? No one said their top regret in life was not accomplishing enough or having been too willing to receive support. Neither of these things was even on the radar. Let this be a reminder to us all.

Culmination

The last of the four phases of the Upward Cycle of Success is Culmination. This phase has the same energy as the luteal phase of your menstrual cycle, the waning moon, and autumn. It's that cozy-sweater-weather-with-a-warm-cup-of-tea energy.

Just this morning I was talking to Licia Morelli, the president of our company, who is also an extraordinary writer. As we discussed how creativity can be seasonal, she realized that she also has a writing season. From December to March, she literally hears the voices of the characters from her stories talking to her and telling her what to write. She spent a long time feeling bad about herself that she doesn't write in the spring and summer. But when she realized that she has a writing season, she was able to embrace it and not waste her energy on spending half the year beating herself up.

I didn't officially start writing this book until October. I don't think it's a coincidence that I began to feel the urge to grab a cup of coffee, close the door to my office, wear knits, light a candle, and really get down to business when the days started to feel noticeably darker, the leaves turned from green to yellow, orange, and red, and there was a bit of a chill in the air. It's because as a whole, the Northern Hemisphere was switching phases into a more inward time of hunkering down and doing the work that can only happen between you and the blank page, the blank canvas, or whatever your particular medium might be.

Now, please don't get caught up in getting too literal about this and thinking that the Upward Cycle of Success of each of your projects should follow the seasons of the year. It doesn't work like that all the time. Sometimes the timeline of a project is much shorter and will go through all four phases in a month. Sometimes it's much longer and will take more than a year. Sometimes it's in between.

I happened to have moved into my first Culmination phase of this book, which was actually putting the words on paper, as summer turned to fall in Maine. (There will be another Culmination phase that happens after the book gets published too, and I'll eventually move into the next

Fertile Void when the next idea begins to gestate. It never ends!)

I like to look at it like this: The menstrual cycle is like the primary piece of your outfit, like a black dress. The cosmic weather, where you are in the Upward Cycle of Success, and what season it is in your part of the world then become accessory items like which sweater or jacket to wear, what shoes to put on, if you're going to wear a scarf or not, and what kind of jewelry you choose.

The foundation is always where your body is—which, of course, you can begin to feel whether or not you're having a cycle. Then the other pieces become additional flavors that you can add to how you invest your time and what you do during your work (or play) day.

The Upward Cycle of Success is designed to help you feel more relaxed and in sync with your own creative process instead of trying to work against yourself and your own creative flow. Instead of the incessant need to be doing something all the time that's become normalized in our "crazy busy" culture, the Upward Cycle of Success reminds us that every phase is productive, even if we're not technically "doing" anything. It reminds us that there's value in rest, that the pause is fertile, and that taking a break is actually time well spent. Because when we embrace all of the seasons and the gifts therein, each season becomes that much more fruitful.

The more you embrace the four distinct phases of creation and the gifts therein, the more you'll uncork your creativity and be astounded by what you're able to make with less effort and little to no agony.

Speaking of less effort, up next is Egg Wisdom. This concept is grounded in your biology and will make your life infinitely easier and more pleasurable to navigate. It's the ultimate "do less, have more" practice.

4

egg wisdom

It was an early spring day in New York, and I was wearing these kind of weird light-wash jeans that were too big for me at the waist and that, due to a tailoring incident, had a raw hem that was just a hair too short. Despite these jeans being weird-looking and far-flung from any trend, I loved them because they felt so good on my body.

I had on the suede Birkenstock clogs I'd bought when I was 16, which I would wear during that time in my life when I wanted to be reminded of what it felt like to be home in Maine. My hair was in a messy ponytail, I wasn't wearing makeup. My outfit was topped off with a tan Patagonia fleece jacket that made me look like a teddy bear because of its clumpy, fuzzy texture and really did nothing for my figure. (Let it be known that I still own these very same jeans, Birkenstock clogs, and Patagonia fleece—and wear them all frequently.)

I'd just dropped my taxes off at my accountant (on time for the first time ever!), and I was feeling really good about myself. This guy stopped me on the street and asked me if I was a dancer. I was a little thrown off and wondered how the heck he knew I was a dancer (at least in a former life) but flattered, nonetheless. He was coming out of a print shop where he was picking up some of his most recent photographs and asked if I'd consider letting him photograph me.

(I understand this sounds like it could have just been a super-creepy line from a super-creepy guy, but my internal guidance is really strong and none of my warning bells were going off.)

I popped into the shop with him to check out his work, and it was beautiful. His eye for light and reflecting women's beauty was striking. So I said yes to being one of his subjects and had the best time with my one experience of being an artist's model.

Have you ever had an experience like this where you haven't put an ounce of energy into your appearance but you randomly get asked out on the street (by someone you'd actually like to go out with) or had someone who's not trying to hit on you simply stop to tell you how radiant you are? Or had a day when all of the lights turn green for you, everyone offers for you to go ahead of them in line, and someone before you pays for your Starbucks at the drive-through?

What you're experiencing here is more than good luck or coincidence. It's a phenomenon I learned about from my mom, Dr. Christiane Northrup, and she calls it Egg Wisdom. I ran an 11-week Egg Wisdom Experience within my membership, Origin, and the women were so enamored with the concept that I thought it deserved an entire chapter.

At its fundamental core, Egg Wisdom is a phenomenon of feminine magnetism that every woman has experienced at least once in her life. Unfortunately, it is often misunderstood, feared, misused, and ignored because we live in a patriarchy that has taught us to devalue or fear that which is not traditionally masculine. But I think it's time for us to reclaim Egg Wisdom because it's one of the key ways that you can have more by doing less.

Now, I'm not an expert in women's reproductive health and anatomy, though I was raised by one. I believe this makes me the perfect person to explain the phenomenon of Egg Wisdom because it's impossible for me to get overly scientific or technical, yet I still have a greater understanding of how it all works below the waist than your average citizen.

Before I get going here, I want you to know that if you identify as a woman, Egg Wisdom applies to you. It doesn't matter if you're postmenopausal, pregnant, or lactating, if you've had a hysterectomy (partial or radical), if you're transgender, or anything else. Egg Wisdom is the *feminine principle* at work, and we all have access to it as long as we understand and employ it.

In order to understand Egg Wisdom, we have to understand how the egg works within the female body. Once a month an egg is released from the ovary (at ovulation) and hangs out for a little bit being available for fertilization.

The egg stays in place right where she is. She doesn't run around up and down the fallopian tube wondering if the sperm is coming to fertilize her. She doesn't pop down to the uterus just to check if he's coming or hang around the cervix entrance, hoping he'll see her there. She doesn't check her phone obsessively or wonder if she should text him or not, even though he didn't respond to her last text (or her last 10). She doesn't call her girlfriends and ask them what they think she should do.

Nope, she simply sits there in all of her fertile eggness, simply being the egg.

As she sits there, though, she also emits a signal that tells the sperm that she's ready and available. The follicular cells around the egg release progesterone, which actually gives the electric currents that drive the movements of the sperms' tails a boost, and as the current increases in strength, the tails begin to move faster.[1]

eggness actually makes the sperm faster and mom says, she has the ability to "egg on" what's around her.

Similarly, when the sperm finds her, there are millions of them trying to break through her barriers to get in all at the same time. But the sperm doesn't get to choose; it's up to the egg who she lets in. Once the egg chooses which sperm (or sperms, in the case of multiples) to let in, if there's anything wrong with its DNA, she actually has the ability to repair its DNA and improve it. Again, she can "egg it on." Then, in order to make the three- to four-day journey down the fallopian tube to the uterus, where the egg will then embed into the uterine lining, she has enough nutrients within her to feed herself and the sperm until they get to the next nutrient source of the uterine wall.

So not only does she have the ability to signal and strengthen the sperm, to choose which one she'll allow to fertilize her, and to repair the sperm's DNA, she also brings a picnic.

This is the feminine way. The feminine nurtures, heals, beautifies, and improves everything around her. Plus, she brings snacks, because someone is always going to be hungry.

If we let the egg be our model of attraction in terms of our very blueprint for how to manifest what we want in life, it gets really juicy, really fun, and a lot less work to get what we want.

If you've ever studied Abraham-Hicks, you're familiar with the concept of allowing. There's the ask for what you want. Then there's the allowing it to come to you. The egg is really good at allowing. She's the perfect leader for us, as women, in what it looks and feels like to allow our desires to come to us.

Because we were taught how to get what we want by a patriarchal culture that always defaults to the lived experience of a man and the masculine way, though, the way of the egg has not been celebrated or taught. In fact, many women I work with tell me that when they take a break or aren't hustling with everything they've got to get what they want, they feel lazy or think they'll never achieve anything.

Let me tell you what. The egg is not lazy. She has the makings of nearly an entire human within her. She's able to repair the DNA of a sperm and also nourish herself and the sperm until they make it to their final destination.

She is not lazy, but she also doesn't waste her precious energy and resources running all around the uterus looking for the sperm or worrying about whether or not it's coming. And by the way, if this month is not her month to be fertilized, she disintegrates within 12 to 24 hours and gets reabsorbed into the female body or simply passes out with your period. She doesn't fight. She doesn't freak out. She lets go and moves on.

I want you to know something for sure: Your body is *wired* for Egg Wisdom. This is not something you need to take a course on or get certified in. You do not need to make 100 vision boards, visualize diligently every single day for 20 minutes, or watch your thoughts like a hawk, having a meltdown every time you think something negative because you think that's broken the spell of attraction.

Nope. When you get off course and you forget to trust, simply be the egg again. It might even help to imagine yourself within a beautiful golden egg sitting in all of your feminine splendor, emitting a signal telling your desire exactly where you are, knowing that your mere presence strengthens your desire's ability to make its way toward you.

This is the wisdom of the egg.

She is who she is. She wants what she wants. She emits a really strong signal, letting what she wants know where she is. She strengthens her desire. She allows her desire in when it arrives. She makes her desire even better as she welcomes it. And then she nourishes her desire as she transforms into the next version of herself.

Now I simply want you to practice being the egg.

I would start with doing it in small ways. If you have a date night coming up with your husband, practice allowing him to please you with whatever the plans are rather than micromanaging everything and booking the reservation yourself, picking the movie, buying the tickets ahead, and getting a babysitter. Maybe lean back and let him do one of those things, or better yet, all of them!

I remember when I was dating a guy back in my twenties in New York City, I really desired him to take the lead more often in our relationship. I was learning about masculine and feminine energy, and I realized how often I was in my masculine energy, making all of the plans, orchestrating everything, and leading the relationship.

At my very core, I think it came from a fear that if I let go I wouldn't get what I wanted. It was a fearful gripping that caused me to be constantly in motion, ready to make happen whatever needed to happen, from paying for the cab to figuring out which street to turn on to planning what we were doing on Saturday night.

Underneath it all, I think I was just afraid of being disappointed. And when I really look at that, I had such an overinflated sense of my capabilities that I didn't give my guy the space to step up. I thought, as so many women do, that if I didn't keep spinning all of the plates and holding the entire world on my shoulders, all of them would come crashing down and the earth would fall out of orbit to its doom.

When I told him one night that I wanted him to take the reins more often in our relationship, he replied that he would love to if I would simply be willing to put them down for a minute.

Touché.

Where does this show up for you? My friend Terri Cole, clinical psychologist and master coach, calls this overfunctioning, and it's super common with high-achieving women, which, if you were attracted to this book, I imagine you are.

Where are you holding on to the reins so tightly that no one else could possibly get ahold of them? Where are you micromanaging the people in your life (or your career) because you have an overinflated idea that no one could possibly do things as well as you do them, or even do the things that you do at all? Where are you doing more than your fair share?

Where could you start practicing being the egg?

It's important to note that being the egg doesn't mean crankily nagging everyone in your family or at work to do things for you. It doesn't mean making requests for support from a place of irritation and disappointment. One way to practice Egg Wisdom is to spend a whole week focusing on appreciation.

Abraham-Hicks says that appreciation has an even more attractive vibration than gratitude because it's purely about noticing what we like about what's in front of us instead of gratitude, which is often about liking what's in front of us as compared to what could be in front of us or what used to be in front of us.

So, for today or the next few days, simply focus on appreciation. What can you find in your immediate environment right now that you can appreciate? For me, it's the way the sun is reflecting off the sequins on a sweet throw pillow my girlfriend gave me that says *hello* on it. It looks magical in the afternoon light as I type this.

I can simultaneously feel an energy of gratitude that my daughter is taking an awesome nap that I know will last another 40 minutes at least. But this is more in contrast to how it used to be when her naps were unpredictable and often lasted only 20 minutes. Do you see the difference?

My feeling about the sequins on the pillow is pure appreciation. How I feel about my daughter napping right now has to do with the moment but more in terms of how this moment relates to a moment in the past and feels better than it used to feel during naptime, when she would wake up screaming at any moment.

Both of these feelings have a place, for sure, but what we want to be shooting for as often as possible is pure appreciation for what's in front of us, as opposed to gratitude for what's in front of us in contrast to how bad it could be or how bad it used to be.

Make sense? It's a quarter turn that will make a world of difference as you practice being the egg.

Simply knowing that your body is wired for Egg Wisdom can often be enough to activate it. Begin to find small ways to do less and be the egg instead. Ask yourself, *What would the egg do or not do?* and then do or don't do what she would do.

You're already preprogrammed for this. Just like making a human, you don't have to think about it. Just be the egg and see what amazing things come swimming toward you!

With Egg Wisdom dialed in, we're now ready to jump into our 14 Do Less Experiments. Each one of these is going to help you tap into a practical way you can feel the true power of having more through doing less in your life. Remember what you've learned about the data supporting doing less, the global evidence for doing less, and the way our cyclical nature supports us in having more through doing less. This isn't the "normal" way to do things, but it is the most sane and wise, and you'll soon see why!

5

introduction to
the experiments

So now we've laid our foundation for what doing less is all about and why it makes sense biologically, sociologically, spiritually, hormonally, and based on real-life data from around the world! Plus, you now understand why women are cyclical beings and how we can embrace this to get into peak creative and productive flow. (Though, once again, productivity is not the Holy Grail here. Sanity is, remember?)

I've told you how I started doing less by accident and then on purpose.

I've told you why doing less is the secret to success for modern women.

I've told you all about the evidence for this so that your left brain can have something to chew on and be satisfied with.

I've told you about the cycles within your body, on our planet, and in the cosmos that support it.

So now it's time to put it all into practice in your life.

These next chapters outline 14 experiments to try out in your own life. If you try out one a day, you've got yourself a two-week program. (But remember: This is not about doing it right or getting an A, so if you miss a day here or there, it so does not matter. Your version of doing less is your version.)

You can try the experiments solo, partner up with a girlfriend, or grab a whole gaggle who want to melt their overwhelm and show up more fully in their lives. Whatever floats your boat.

Now, let me be super-duper clear. This is NOT about being perfect. It's not about executing every experiment with precision and getting a perfect 10.0 from the Olympic judge.

This is simply about seeing what happens if every day, in small ways, we practice doing less than we might usually do.

This is not about doing nothing either. Some people hear about my do less philosophy and immediately go into massive resistance.

How the heck does she expect my family to not fall apart if I do less? How am I going to run my household? My career will fall apart. My kids will go hungry and become feral. My marriage will collapse. The whole neighborhood will go to pot, and quite frankly, I wouldn't be surprised if the entire world comes crashing down if I do less.

Yeah, I get it. We've been programmed to believe that the only way to live is to stay in action at all times. We talked all about that in Chapters 1 and 3. I'd like to remind you that our obsession with action and productivity is *programming*.

Here's the truth: You've likely not tried doing less before unless you were sick to the point of having to give up and do less as a total and complete last resort because you couldn't get off the couch without a pounding headache, throwing up, or running to the bathroom with diarrhea.

So if you're feeling resistance right now, there are two things I want to say: It's totally normal, and it makes sense. I too was skeptical and thought that the well-being of the world depended on me staying in constant motion unless I was sleeping (and even then I'd better be ready to get going quickly should anything need doing).

Still, if you haven't tried doing less before, how do you

know what will happen?

That is the point of these experiments. I'm not asking you to overhaul your life. I'm not asking you to do less forever. I'm simply asking you to try each of the following experiments of different ways to do less in your life and see what happens.

Of course, as a fellow do less researcher myself, I also want to hear how it goes for you. I want to know what kind of results you experience, how you feel, how the people in your life react, and what shifts you notice in your family and work life. I also want to know what it feels like to be with yourself when you're doing less.

As you go through the following chapters and experiments, please share your findings with me on Instagram using the hashtag #DoLess. We are all pioneers in this great frontier of doing life as working mothers differently, and none of us needs to be out here on our own. We've got to stick together.

Onward to the experiments!

PART II

the
do less
experiments

experiment

1

track your
cycle and the moon

I told you earlier how devastated I was when I got my period for the first time. I did not look at this as a welcomed rite of passage into womanhood. I saw it as the end of my childhood, which I didn't feel ready to be done with.

I got my period on the relatively early side. I was one of the very first of my circle of close friends, and it was super heavy, which made the whole thing entirely inconvenient.

Despite my mom having written "the Bible of women's health," I really wasn't open to hearing about the wisdom of the menstrual cycle and the gifts it offered to me. I just figured out how to manage it, had to call home every now and again to get picked up after leaking through my pants and feeling very grateful I had a sweater to wrap around my waist, and that was that. I barely ever knew when my period was coming and was perpetually caught off guard when it arrived, having to borrow a tampon from a friend or run to the nearest drugstore.

I didn't hate my period, as beyond some cramps on day one and day four and the heavy bleeding, it didn't impede me living my life, particularly. But I certainly didn't love it or welcome it in any way. I was indifferent with a slight leaning toward annoyed by it.

While I didn't give my mom the opportunity to mark the rite of passage of my first period with any fanfare (as she would have preferred), my next major life milestone gave us both the opportunity to celebrate together. I was getting married, and I needed a dress.

We bought the first wedding dress I tried on when I went dress shopping with my mom on a whim a few weeks after I'd gotten engaged. It fit perfectly, and I cried the minute I saw my reflection in the mirror.

But when I tried the dress on six months later, it wouldn't zip because I'd put on some pounds. I panicked, and some old and not-so-healthy programming got triggered around my body and having grown up a little chubbier than my friends, occasionally being teased on the playground by the other kids ("Move it, fatso" and that kind of thing).

I went on an extremely intense diet and exercise program where I weighed every single bite of food that went into my mouth and counted my proteins, fats, and carbs for four months plus worked out seven days a week for up to two hours at a time.

The result? My dress was too big for me on the day of the wedding. I'd lost 20 pounds and was the skinniest I'd ever been. In addition to 20 pounds, I also lost my period. A month after the wedding, when I was still counting my macros and working out intensely, my mom looked at me and said, "Honey. That is not a fertile body." Even after I came to my senses, it still took four months for my period to come back.

Mike and I then somewhat spontaneously decided to try to conceive, and we were so blessed that it worked the first time! So, besides the one cycle, between getting really skinny, being pregnant, and then nursing, I didn't have my period for over two years.

I had read both the menstruation chapter in *Women's Bodies, Women's Wisdom* and also Alisa Vitti's entire book, *WomanCode*, both of which are quite illuminating as to the inherent wisdom of the menstrual cycle and how it can be such a beautiful guide for women in leading the rhythm of their lives and creativity. Yet, for whatever reason, I didn't get how truly amazing this thing was that had been going on in my body since I was 12 without me even having to think about it, and that was the foundation for me being able to create a human inside my body, until it went away for over two years.

When my period came back, it was as though with it came a downloaded blueprint about how cool the menstrual cycle is as a guide for living a sustainable life. I then started tracking my cycle pretty religiously.

I learned later from Dr. Louann Brizendine in *The Female Brain* that one of the greatest predictors of maternal thriving is predictability. Yet motherhood has been the most unpredictable thing I've experienced. The lack of predictability and lack of being able to control next to anything has been the thing that I've struggled with the most (to the point of turning into a total sleep-training drill sergeant and developing postpartum insomnia, which I'll tell you about more later).

So when I read Brizendine's chapter on the Mommy Brain and how we, as mothers, need to have some areas of our life where we know what to expect (mainly resources and support), it was a eureka moment. First of all, I understood so deeply why I had struggled so much with the lack of predictability, especially in the first year of motherhood, and second, why I was getting so much satisfaction from tracking my menstrual cycle now that it was back.

Before becoming a mother, my life was pretty much within my control. In fact, I'd done everything in my power to ensure that no one else had much of a say at all as to how I spent my time, where I went, or when.

I'd devoted my whole career to finding more ways to create freedom, especially financially and career-wise, and teaching others what I'd learned. So suddenly being held hostage to the vagaries of a tiny person who couldn't even tell me what she needed and would just cry and cry and cry and not sleep was borderline torturous to me.

It makes sense to me, in retrospect, why tracking my cycle had never been a priority. I decided when I woke up, when I went to sleep, where I went during the day, what projects I worked on, who I hung out with, who I dated, where I traveled and when, what I spent money on, and really everything else. So I didn't need the predictability of knowing when my period was coming and when I was going to experience the four phases of my cycle. I had a vague recollection that there were four phases and that each of them had a particular energetic gift and focus, but it felt complicated to pay attention and like something that only women who had problematic periods needed to do.

Cut to me many years later treating my period as a gift. You see, our patriarchal culture has blamed women for being unpredictable for thousands of years, using this as evidence as to why women could not be in positions of power or be part of important decision-making processes.

The term *hysteria* (from the Greek *hystera*, meaning "uterus") was first used by Hippocrates back in the fifth century as a catchall for basically every physical and mental ailment women experienced, including sexual forwardness. It wasn't until 1980 that the diagnosis was officially done away with by the American Psychiatric Association, and it was still used well through the 20th century to label all kinds of mental afflictions that women experienced.[1]

In ancient Greece, they actually thought the uterus could move about within the body. "Wandering uterus" was believed to be the cause of all women's problems (aka hysteria) and the reason men used to keep women from participating in public life. Labeling every affliction women had as hysteria and linked to the mere fact of being born a woman for millennia is only one of the ways that the patriarchy has squashed feminine power—because one of the most powerful things about us is our menstrual cycles and our ability to create humans.

When I began to track my cycle and find tremendous solace in the predictability of the four phases, I realized that women are incredibly predictable in a cyclical way. No, we don't operate on a 24-hour cycle like men do. But that doesn't make us wrong. It simply makes us different from the default male standard that everything in our society has been based on for far too long.

We cycle in an incredibly predictable, 28-ish day way, and while we're not the same within the span of every day, we are quite predictable within the span of every month. And what's even more awesome is that, as we discussed in Chapter 3, each of our distinct four phases has tremendous gifts for our creativity and our entire lived experience of being a woman.

And whether you're cycling or not, our experience of living on planet Earth is influenced by the 28-day cycle of the moon. It's predictable. The same four phases happen with each trip around the earth. It's there for us at all times, to remind us that we don't need to be robots, performing the same way every day, but that, in fact, there's a beautiful, meaningful, wise ebb and flow happening around us at all times that's available to tap into whenever we desire extra guidance and a structure to live in that's alternative to the 24/7 "push, push, push, hustle, hustle, hustle" model that we've all been taught.

I not only started tracking when my period was estimated to start, something I'd already done off and on for years, I added in tracking when I was moving from one phase of my cycle to the next. This was the gold mine for me.

Our health teachers leave out all of the awesome information about our periods when we learn about it in late elementary or middle school. They tell us that we bleed once a month, and it has to do with our ability to get pregnant. Period.

But that's not all of it at all! That's not the period! They miss out on telling us about all of the beauty of it and all of the gifts that are totally unique to the lived experience of a woman. (I don't blame our health teachers. Chances are pretty good they are as ignorant as their students are of anything to talk about other than the bleeding part.)

When I really gave over to learning about the four phases and how I could organize my life around how I felt depending on which phase I was in, it was like I had found this gigantic, beautiful room inside my home, filled with all of my most favorite things and decorated exactly to my style, that I'd never known about.

I'd been sitting on the perfect way to organize my life, my projects, and my energy my whole life and never even knew. But the cool thing is that once you know something, you can never unknow it. So I dove in.

I started taking note of which day of my cycle I was on, which phase of my cycle I was in, and how I felt each day in a notebook before bed. I only wrote a few sentences. It didn't take much time. But I was using myself as my laboratory, and it felt so good to know how I felt throughout the month and to stop blaming myself for not feeling perky, energized, and ready to take on the world every single day of every single month.

Now I knew that the days I had lower energy, had trouble focusing, and just wanted to lie in bed all day were just as valuable as the days I could write 2500 words in an hour and still have energy left over to work out, do an interview, play with my daughters, and make dinner for my family. What was even more revolutionary was that I began to honor the days I wanted to lie low and not try to force myself to do activities that I wasn't hormonally or energetically poised to do!

I also added in tracking the moon to this whole shebang because I thought it added an interesting flavor. How did I feel if I was bleeding on the full moon as opposed to the new moon? What was my energy like? How was my intuition? What was my focus like? How much did I want to nap? Was I irritable?

I approached it from the perspective of gathering data, and that's what made it so effective. I wasn't approaching it from a place of trying to fix myself or compare myself to a gold standard of what the perfect experience of a cycle would be. Nope. I was simply tracking my lived experience of being me, one example of a cyclical woman living on planet Earth.

This daily practice of tracking my cycle not only became my primary tool for planning my days, it also became the blueprint for the Daily Energy Tracker that over 1,000 of our Origin members and Origin Planner users use every day to gather their own data about their own lives.

So often we hear about the importance and power of loving yourself in the personal development world. And so often we have no idea what it means to love ourselves. *What does that even look like? Can I get something a little more concrete?*

As I began to track my cycle, the result of the most feminine part of myself, my reproductive system, my self-compassion and self-love grew by leaps and bounds. I realized that this was the most practical way that I could love myself, and specifically my body. No other self-love practice even held a candle to the depth of understanding and honoring that I developed through the daily practice of tuning in to how my body felt, paying attention to where she was in her cycle and in her dance with the moon, and then adjusting the way I invested my time as a result.

Practical as anything. Effective as hell.

So that's your first experiment. Track your cycle, not just the day you think you're going to start bleeding so you can make sure you have a tampon in your purse, but the whole enchilada. The whole gorgeous thing. All four phases.

If you're not cycling, you can track the moon. And, honestly, even if you are, I *highly* recommend getting yourself a lunar calendar and tracking the full moon, the new moon, and ideally the waxing quarter and the waning quarter in conjunction with your own menstrual cycle.

Tracking my cycle has made me feel so held by something greater than myself, and when I started I felt like I was really doing things right in a more profound way than I'd ever experienced. The lived experience of finding my body right, no matter what she was experiencing on any given day, was one of the most healing transformations I've ever had the pleasure of undergoing.

And you, my dear, have access to that very same healing immediately.

There are new apps coming out every day that can help you track your cycle right on your smartphone. I recommend trying out a few to find the one that really works for you. A few to check out are Kindara, Glow, Clue, and MyFlo.

I also love my Daily Energy Tracker, which I created for our Origin ladies. You can access it by checking out the Appendix or going to katenorthrup.com/gifts to download it so you can print it out and use it.

Now, how is tracking your cycle going to help you do less?

Well, what's so cool about your cycle (or the lunar phases) is that it will tell you what you need to be focusing on during each week so that you don't have to wonder what to prioritize or if you're doing the right thing. Also, you don't need to waste your precious time and energy pushing yourself to do tasks and projects that you don't have the energy for during this particular phase.

There is no time management system on earth that's actually based on the lived experience of being female, of being cyclical in a 28-day cycle instead of a 24-hour cycle. That's why if you've tried every time management system but have yet to find one that doesn't simply leave you scrambling, you feel like you're still always just running out of time and must be hopelessly disorganized.

But if you let your body lead the way, she knows what's best for you, *and* you'll find you're wildly productive. (This is a totally awesome side benefit of honoring the vessel that's holding your soul for this particular trip as a human.)

Start by tracking your cycle and figuring out when you'll be in each phase. Then, simply start to plan your time to a small degree so that you'll be focused on the following during each phase.

- Follicular/waxing crescent: Planning, brainstorming, and new beginnings

- Ovulation/full moon: Communicating, collaborating, attracting, being out there

- Luteal/waning crescent: Focus, details, finishing projects, putting in the work

- Menstrual/new moon: Rest, reflection, and evaluation

At first you'll likely only be able to add a slight flavor of each of these phases to the given week you're in because things are planned far in advance and it takes a while to get synced up. But over time you'll want to move toward having 20 to 25 percent of your activities be ideal for the given phase you're in.

When you plan your time this way, you'll be amazed by how much less stress you feel, how much more you get done in a shorter period of time, and how much less energy you waste trying to not only fit yourself into a mold that wasn't designed for you, but also to get yourself to do things that you don't feel like doing.

What's so ingenious about the design of your cyclical nature is that there's a time during the 28 days that's perfect for every kind of task that you might need to do within that time frame. And if you simply schedule the type of task for the energy of the phase it's most suited for, your life works a lot better, your body feels way better, and you're no longer living at odds with who you are. Instead, you're honoring yourself with every appointment you make, every scheduling choice you make, and every calendar entry.

What I've found is that simply putting my attention on a particular area of my life enhances it in really beautiful ways, so the act of tracking your cycle may very well begin to heal your cycle and make your life feel more predictable and beautiful without you having to do anything else!

Give it a go and report back on this experiment using the hashtag #DoLess on social media if you care to share publicly and with me!

2

discover
what really
matters to you

If you ask most people what really matters to them, they'll tell you some combination of their family, their friends, perhaps their faith or spirituality, the earth, their health, and being of service. But if most of us take an honest look at our schedules, what we spend our time on doesn't reflect the things that we say matter to us.

The whole purpose of doing less is to have the experience of having more. Not more *stuff*, but more *meaning* in our lives.

When we're chasing goals, it's ultimately because we think achieving those things is going to make us feel a certain way, usually a way that makes us feel like our life is meaningful and fulfilling. If you're looking for more soulful guidance for calling in what you desire that doesn't just tell you to dig in and work harder, I recommend checking out *Emergent Strategy* by Adrienne Maree Brown, *Own Your Glow* by Latham Thomas, and *The Alchemist* by Paulo Coelho.

Now, I can get caught up in our cultural obsession with achievement and racing toward a nonexistent finish line as much as the next lady, but what I've found really helps me focus on what really matters is reverse engineering my life based on what matters to me most.

If you don't ever stop to ask yourself what really matters to you, you'll unconsciously organize your life around filling it with the things that matter the most to your parents or the things that matter the most to our culture as a whole. And you'll never actually get the chance to live your own life, which is very sad indeed.

I remember one particular year I was attending international convention, wearing a cocktail dress in heels that hurt my feet but made my legs look amazing, surrounded by the top achievers in the direct sales company that my husband and I partner with (and actually met through). We were being recognized for our achievements that year, but I didn't feel like we'd done enough. Instead of being in the top 25 growers, we were in the top 100. We hadn't focused on our business the way we would have needed to in order to really be amongst the crème de la crème of performers.

I was feeling kind of bad about it. I was sitting there all dolled up, beating myself up for not having spent the past year pushing harder, working more hours, talking to more people, presenting more often, and generally putting in more effort. It wasn't that I wasn't proud of what we'd accomplished, it was that I felt obsessed that we should have done more because I knew we *could* have done more.

When I shared how I was feeling with Mike later on, though, and we really talked through the entire past year and what felt the best in our lives and what we were really proud of, we realized that all of our priorities were totally in the right place.

We'd had a gorgeous wedding, which many of our friends shared was incredibly meaningful for them on a personal level aside from the joy they'd experienced celebrating us. We'd really put down beautiful roots in Maine and had a supportive community we loved. Our relationship was really strong, and we were going on amazing adventures together all the time. We'd had some difficult but important healing within our families in the past year. And we'd had some business successes that we were proud of too.

I suddenly realized that each summer we would come to the convention and I would be overcome with a feeling that I wasn't doing enough. I would start to feel behind, unfocused, and like I didn't have enough to show for the past year going by.

The feeling of not having done enough would begin to sink in a few weeks before the convention and would last as a hangover for a couple of months afterward, usually motivating me to be in super-massive action mode right after we got home, but then petering out as life got under way and other priorities began to rise to the surface.

During the conversation with Mike, it became abundantly clear that I no longer needed to succumb to the "not-doing-enough blues," because when I really got honest with myself, the reality of my life and what I was putting my attention on was totally in alignment with what really matters to me:

- My relationship with myself and my body

- My relationship with God/Goddess/the Universe

- My relationship with Mike (and now our kids)

- My relationship with my family

- My relationship with our community

- My relationship with and stewardship of the earth

- My relationship with our business and being of service —uplifting women and girls

When I sat down to write out what really mattered to me, like what I would be thinking about if I only had a few months to live and what I would want to focus on, I realized that being a top achiever or earner in our direct sales company wasn't even close to the top of the list. It felt soooooo good to let my yearly angst and self-flagellation go that year, and I'm happy to report that they haven't returned.

Now I attend our annual event, and while I'm always happy to celebrate achievements and milestones, I don't get caught up in comparing myself to others or blaming myself for all of the things I could have done but didn't do throughout the year. Instead I focus on meaningful connections with our team and greater community within the company, on learning new things, and on being present.

The energy I spent beating myself up for a few months every year can now either be invested in actually growing that part of our business if that's what feels right at the time, or in something else that's made it onto the list of things that mean the most to me.

In my book, energy saved is always time saved. Why? Because when you're leaking your energy into beating yourself up, beating someone else up, trying to change someone, or trying to do something that doesn't actually matter to you, you not only have less energy for what does matter to you, you also have a tendency to have trouble focusing, to lose your creative edge, and to feel uninspired. When you're investing energy in things that don't ultimately matter to you, life loses its luster. You begin to wonder what's wrong with you and if this is really it.

All of that wasted energy sucks the life out of your time too. Days and weeks go by when you can't get any traction. And instead of simply surrendering to that fact (because sometimes you're just in a fallow period and embracing it is the best option), you fight it the whole time, making you more tired and even less invested in the life you're living.

Recently I was at a business conference with a girlfriend who's in a similar business to mine. We sat on a velvet banquette in the lobby of an elegant hotel watching beautiful people pass by as we immediately dropped into the grit of our lives.

She was tired. She'd been busting her ass all year. She'd developed a chronic virus that she couldn't seem to heal.

"What are we doing all of this for, anyway?" she asked me, halfway joking but really more serious than not. The social media, the speaking, the publishing, the products, the launches, the programs. She'd lost track of what it all meant.

"I don't know," I replied, "but I know that I love posting and connecting with my community on Instagram and I love writing my blog every week. I would do both even if they had nothing to do with our business. They fill me up."

Connection and expression. That's what it boils down to for me. Am I telling the truth in a way that's helpful for other people? Am I connecting with other humans in a meaningful way on a regular basis? The rest is just details.

So, this next experiment I'd like you to try out is to identify what really matters to you. You could write it down on a Post-it note, the back of a takeout menu that's lying around your kitchen, in the Notes section on your phone, in your journal, or wherever. But please do write it down.

(If you want to be inspired by how crystal clear you can get when it comes to what matters to you, read Tiffany Dufu's book *Drop the Ball*. Her personal list in Chapter 7 is specific and awe-inspiring—as is the whole book.)

The awareness of what matters to you will begin to create seismic shifts in your life without you having to do much else. That's what's so cool about awareness. It often does a whole boatload of the work for us (yay for doing less!).

If you want to take your awareness even further, take a look at your calendar from the past three months or so. How many of the appointments, meetings, and other things you spent your time on were in service to the things you identified as meaningful to you? How much of your time was spent on things that are not on the list of what's most meaningful to you?

While this experiment may seem really basic and obvious, I find that unless I'm super vigilant, my time will get sucked away by the gremlins of that which has no meaning for me.

I have to diligently stand at the gateway of my time and be very discerning about what makes it onto my schedule and what doesn't. If I schedule my life by default, my days will very quickly be taken up by the things that matter to other people but aren't necessarily at the top of the list for me. And how we spend our days is ultimately how we spend our lives.

I don't want to be lying on my deathbed wishing that I'd invested my time in the things that mattered to me instead of frittering it away trying to make other people happy and keep up with my neighbors or the strangers I follow on the Internet, or on things that ended up in my life because I just wasn't paying that close attention.

No. I want the vast majority of my time to be invested in enhancing the things that matter to me. Period. End of story.

Looking over my schedule at the beginning of each week and seeing if what's on there is in service to what truly matters to me is a weekly gatekeeping behavior that I highly recommend adopting if you too want to live a meaningful life.

Naturally, the ideal outcome of identifying what matters to you and looking back over your recent schedule to see how much of what you're doing with your time aligns is that over time you move toward 100 percent of your time being invested in the things that matter the most to you.

If you're a Perfectionistic Polly, you may use this as an opportunity to beat yourself up for not doing well enough at keeping the things that don't matter to you off your schedule. Using your time and energy this way would also not be in alignment with what matters to you, though, so be careful.

None of us will ever get to 100 percent of our time invested in the things that matter the most to us. I think shooting for 80 percent would be awesome. Just as an airplane that's set for a specific direction never is 100 percent perfectly heading there, we always need to be course correcting, pointing our nose back toward what matters.

You'll never get there. It will never be done. Every day is a clean slate. That's why this is called an experiment.

experiment

3

listen to your body

When I was pregnant with our first daughter, Penelope, my body asked me to slow waaaay down to a pace that I'd never given myself permission to operate within.

I had so much inner chatter bubble up about my worth and what people would think and if I was lazy or not and was I pulling my weight at home and in my business and if my husband was going to resent me and who did I think I was for taking it easy while I was creating a human being inside my womb. At times the noise was deafening. But it was like pus rising to the surface to be extracted. That nine months of my body asking me very loudly to rest and me (mostly) responding by giving it to her was a huge healing and reprogramming for me around my previous tendency to stay in action as a way to prove my worth.

At the end of that year when we looked at our financials I was shocked to find that our business had remained steady as opposed to having tanked. Plus, we had a beautiful baby girl in our arms! Being her and (later) her sister's conduit into the world is by far the most productive thing I've ever done in my life, but on the outside it looked like I was doing a whole lotta *nothing*. It was hard to wrap my head around.

No action to be seen. HUGE result.

There's no way of knowing what would have happened had I not had the freedom or wisdom to listen when my body was asking me to rest and slow down throughout the entire pregnancy, but I have a strong sense that I might not have had such a healthy pregnancy or easeful recovery as I had— physically speaking, anyway. Emotionally I struggled, as I've already shared with you.

I remember going on my first diet when I was 11 years old. I dieted on and off throughout my entire life until I got pregnant. It was the first time that my body very loudly told me what she needed and because I figured there was someone other than me who needed what my body was asking for, whose survival, in fact, depended on it, I'd better listen.

All through pregnancy I ate what my body asked for and stopped when I was full (something I'd struggled to do my whole life up until that point). I moved or didn't move the way she wanted. It was the wildest experience to know so clearly what she needed and to, for the first time I could remember, not question it based on what I knew about nutrition or calories or body fat or the prevention or burning thereof. I just did what she asked.

While I was nursing it was the same. I had moments where I wanted to slip into my old habits of going on a program or a cleanse because the lack of strict rules made me feel a little uneasy, at times, and there was a part of me that craved the control of someone else telling me what I could and couldn't eat. But for the first time, my body was telling me what I could and couldn't eat and she was loud and really hard to ignore. During pregnancy, my body asked for ramen noodles all the time (specifically from this amazing place in Portland, Maine, called Pai Men Miyake, that I highly recommend if you ever come to town—try the Shojin). Then, while I was nursing, she wanted potato chips, specifically the Kettle brand sea salt ones. I'd never been much of a potato chip girl, but I think I went through four bags a week in the early months of motherhood.

Logically speaking, potato chips are not a nutrient-dense food, and certainly not the way to go if you're wanting to head in the direction of getting smaller rather than bigger. But the craving for chips wasn't coming from a place of emotional emptiness or stress where I was trying to cover something I didn't want to feel with salt and fat. Nope, it felt really different. The feeling I had about wanting potato chips felt very visceral, like totally primal. It was a very clean feeling, unsullied by my emotional needs.

I knew the desire for certain foods during pregnancy and nursing was different from eating my emotions because I almost never overate. When I was done, I was done. I didn't need to sit and debate with myself about whether or not to have another handful. I was done and that was that.

After spending my high school and adult years up to that point reading every new diet and nutrition book and trying all the different programs and cleanses I heard of, listening to what my body wanted food-wise (and rest- and movement-wise) was revolutionary. I no longer needed to look outside myself for a set of rules to follow. I didn't need to check in with someone else. I didn't need to question my desires. I felt what I wanted, and then I gave it to my body.

And while I assumed that eating bowls of potato chips and trail mix made with M&M's in the middle of the night while nursing would have significantly slowed my body reorganizing herself after birth, I was able to heal really beautifully and had a body shape and size I felt really good about within 10 months of giving birth without having to try.

Yes, I moved my body regularly and didn't go through the McDonald's drive-through for my meals, but I didn't go on a diet, start a new fitness regime, count any calories, cut out any food groups (except for when I found out Penelope was allergic to them), or really do anything at all other than listen to my body.

As a result, my body regained her strength and her new shape. (I really hate to say "getting the body back," because there's really no going backward after birth and I think our cultural fixation with getting your body back after baby is just a hair short of insanity.) All of this happened on its own, with me simply following instructions.

When I stopped nursing Penelope, she was 18 months old and I vowed to not lose the connection to my body's clear desires even though I was now feeding only myself for the first time in 2 years and 3 months (the months of pregnancy plus 18 months of nursing). I wish I could report back that it was just as easy to hear what my body wanted when I was only responsible for nourishing myself, but I would be lying.

Luckily, every time I started Googling nutrition programs or cleanses or was tempted to get on the bandwagon of someone else making the rules for my body, I had a stop valve that would trigger and remind me that my best guide was with me all the time. She'd managed to nourish one beautiful child for two years and three months while keeping me healthy at the same time. Certainly she could guide me in what to put in my mouth and how she wanted to move even if my body wasn't responsible for feeding someone else anymore (at least not until I got pregnant again four months after I stopped nursing).

Those four months were key, though, because they allowed me to practice turning up the volume on what my body wanted.

I tried intermittent fasting for a couple of months because I was waking up feeling super sluggish and I thought it might help me boost my energy. It worked wonderfully at first and then all of a sudden I started having digestive issues and being constipated. She was speaking pretty loudly again, so I stopped the intermittent fasting, started adding more veggies into my diet, and felt great again, just in time to get pregnant with baby number two. I didn't need someone to tell me when the fasting wasn't working for me anymore. My body told me.

The take-home message is this: Our bodies are sending us signals all the time. They come via our energy levels, via how well we're sleeping, via what's going on with our cycle, with our immune system, with our digestion, with our skin, and more.

We have a choice: listen when we get the signal the first time or ignore it until it gets louder, usually in the form of an illness we can no longer ignore because it's completely knocked us out.

This isn't just a "spiritual" idea either. A study in the journal *Biological Psychology* suggests that those who have better body awareness experience less stress.[1] Doesn't matter who you are, working mama or not. We all could stand to feel less frazzled, right?

I have found that if I listen the first time, getting to the root of what's ailing me, physically, emotionally, spiritually, or otherwise, just doesn't take as long. Getting sick just doesn't feel like a good use of my time. How about you?

Now, our bodies don't only give us signals about what to eat, how they want to move, when we need a break, or if something we're ingesting or a way we're ingesting it isn't working for us. They also tell us all kinds of other super-useful information, like when certain people rub us the wrong way, when we should bail on a project, when to say yes, when to say no, which direction to head, and more.

However, most people weren't raised to listen to their bodies as their primary source of wisdom. Nope. They were raised to listen to their parents or other authority figures as their primary source of wisdom and instruction, so getting back in touch with the messages your body has been sending all along can take a little practice.

Don't feel bad if you don't know how to listen to your body or if you didn't even know that she's been talking to you this whole time. Like I said before, while the best time to start doing something was always yesterday, the second-best time to start is today! And the good news is that it's today! So you're just in time.

When you listen to your body, you end up needing to do way less wondering if you're doing the right thing when it comes to nutrition or exercise, relationships, your career, your mothering, or really any other category of your life you can think of. It saves you time and energy from thinking about things endlessly, from consulting your friends for advice, from consulting experts for advice, and from getting sick because you didn't listen.

Listening to your body may be one of the best ways to save time and energy you'll ever come across. It's also a way of being an activist.

What do I mean by that? Well, just under the surface of the interactions between men, women, and children everywhere runs the energy of rape culture. To state it more bluntly, it's been historically acceptable for people, specifically men, to do whatever they want regarding a woman's body regardless of her consent. Luckily with the history of sexual harassment and assault from public figures like Harvey Weinstein, Kevin Spacey, Mario Batali, Matt Lauer, Charlie Rose, Bill Cosby, Donald Trump, and Louis C.K., to name just a few, being uncovered and in many cases leading to prosecution, this culture is shifting.

While I completely agree that we need to hold men accountable for their behavior and raise boys to respect women and teach both boys and girls about consent, it also needs to change within us as grown women. How can we expect men to listen to our consent and respect our bodies if we are not listening to the needs of our own bodies on a daily basis? How can we teach our daughters how to care for themselves, keep themselves safe, and tap into their power if we're spending every day ignoring our bodies' yeses and nos?

One of history's most powerful feminist poets and activists, Audre Lorde, said it best: "Caring for myself is not self-indulgence, it is self-preservation, and that is an act of political warfare."

Culture is not "out there"; it is made up of each and every one of *us*. So if we want to change the culture, we have to change ourselves. Honoring our bodies and respecting their yeses and nos is an incredibly powerful way to do that. If we want to end violence against women and girls worldwide, let's start with ourselves.

So, of course, this next Do Less Experiment is to listen to your body.

What do I mean by that? Well, you can give it a go right now. Close your eyes and simply tune in to how your body feels. Is there any pain, discomfort, or tension in your body? Where is it located? How big is it? If it had a color, what would it be? If it had a message for you, what would it say?

The key here is not to think but instead to *feel* and *listen*. The information you get might not seem logical, but that's just your analytical brain trying to stay in control.

Some people will get their messages as feelings. Some will get them as clear words almost as though they've heard them (and some will actually hear voices). And some will get their messages as pictures, which might be literal or might be symbolic. Sometimes the message you get is crystal clear and sometimes it's hazy. That's okay too. Your body takes as long as it wants to take to tell you what you need to know.

The key here is to keep listening, every day, so that your body knows that you're actually available. When she really feels that you're available to hear what she has to share with you, she'll start giving you more information because she feels safe and heard.

Sound familiar? Aren't we more likely to open up to someone when we feel safe and heard? Your body is no different.

Another great listening to your body exercise is to simply ask a straightforward question. I would start with something you already know the answer to so you can begin to feel what a yes feels like within your body and what a no feels like.

You could start with something like *Is my name _____?* and use your actual name. Close your eyes, ask the question, and then feel what you feel.

Then try the opposite and ask, *Is my name _____?* and use a name that's not your name. Close your eyes as you ask and then feel what you feel.

For me, a yes feels like an expansion. It feels like I get more space inside my body.

A no feels like a contraction and like the inside of my body is getting darker and more compact. I often get a tightening in my stomach or a feeling of slight anxiety for a no, especially when it comes to asking if I should move forward with a particular project or collaboration with someone.

My husband and I recently realized that one of the biggest reasons we've been able to create a really solid, abundant business in a relatively short period of time is that we make decisions relatively quickly. We don't need to think about things for weeks on end and consult a bunch of experts or friends or colleagues. We know what feels right.

We know what doesn't feel right. We simply act on how it feels *in our bodies.*

I have yet to get a bum steer when I'm really heeding my body's advice.

Sometimes the information comes abruptly, like when I decided to stop nursing my first daughter. Our nursing relationship was working until all of a sudden it wasn't. I'd read all kinds of advice and stories about how to wean gradually because I knew it was on the horizon, but I wasn't ready yet. When people would ask me how long I planned to nurse (which, by the way, was none of their business), I would respond that I would stop when it was clear that either I was done or that Penelope was done.

I was done first, and the information came as a wave of pure knowing as I sat and nursed her for the last time in an office chair with my feet propped up on a desk in the spare room where my in-laws keep a crib for the grandkids. The wave of bittersweet emotion I felt was intense. I looked into her eyes as tears streamed out of mine and simply all of a sudden knew.

The next morning my husband and I left for a four-day trip to British Columbia, and Penelope stayed in Indiana with her Mimi and Pappa. I bawled all the way to the airport and let the grief I felt about being finished nursing Penelope wash over me. My husband simply listened and let me feel my feelings.

Just because my body knew the truth didn't make it all rainbows and unicorns. I was still sad. I still had doubt. I still experienced a feeling of deep loss even though I knew it was right.

It's not always going to be information that feels really great to hear. Sometimes you'd rather not know what you know. But your body always knows, and if you don't listen to her, she will find another way until you finally do, so why not practice daily? You can ask her what you should wear, what to do for your workout that day, and what to have for lunch to start strengthening the connection.

Then, as you begin to hear what she has to say really clearly around smaller things like your outfit and your meal choice, you can start to ask about bigger things like new offerings in your business, whether or not to hire a sleep coach for your wakeful one-year-old, if you should confront your mother about that thing she keeps doing that's driving you crazy, and whether or not to collaborate with your friend on that project she invited you to work on.

When you listen to your body and heed what she says—at least most of the time, because no one is perfect and we all have our defiant days when we just can't help but follow our ego—you will:

- Do less wondering if you're doing the right thing.

- Spend less time consulting other people to make decisions.

- Spend less time making decisions, period.

- Spend less time being sick.

- Spend less time backtracking from decisions that you wish you hadn't made in the first place.

Bottom line: Listening to what your body has to say is a HUGE time and energy saver.

Give it a go and please report back!

experiment

4

check your vitals

When I was in the hospital after Penelope was born, I not only felt like I was in baby jail, I felt so unbelievably violated by nurses coming in all day and all night to monitor Penelope's and my vitals. When you take two people and factor in that you're getting checked on every two hours, it was simply way too many people coming in and out of our room. No matter how aggravating I may have found it as a patient, however, knowing my blood pressure, temperature, etc., was critical information for the medical staff to ensure that Penelope and I were stable.

When it comes to your health, there are a vital few things that need to be focused on that are a foundation to your whole body working. In your life and business, there are a vital few things that you and you alone need to be doing in order to keep the train moving and have the greatest impact. Yet most of us spend the vast majority of our lives focusing on *everything*—and therefore really never focusing on anything, especially not the vital things.

If the nurses in the hospital came in every two hours and measured *every* single health factor imaginable, it would take forever and be a huge waste of time. They wouldn't get the bang for their buck that they do when they gauge how well a patient is doing based on a few key factors.

I learned about the concept of identifying your "vital few" in business from Darren Hardy, publisher of *Success* magazine, and it changed the way I operated from the moment I implemented this philosophy. In fact, I'm quite sure that identifying and focusing on my vital few in business was a large part of the reason why our business didn't tank when I was pregnant, or during the first year of Penelope's life, when we were exhausted and simply trying to keep our noses above the water.

If you've ever heard of the Pareto principle, or the 80/20 rule, then the idea of the vital few will be easy to grasp. The two concepts can be used in tandem to keep you between the ditches and focused on what matters most during the precious hours that you have.

The 80/20 rule says that 80 percent of your results will come from 20 percent of your actions. Kind of a bummer and liberating all at the same time, because you realize how much time you must be wasting and you realize how little you might actually need to put in effort in order to get the results that you want.

Similarly, your vital few are the few things (we're talking about three things here) that you and *only* you can do in your work life that move the needle forward the most in terms of getting you closer to your goals, driving revenue, or whatever other measure of success is appropriate.

I was able to identify my vital few as creating content and connecting with people in a meaningful way (like at events or with my online community on Facebook Live as examples). So really, I have a vital *two*, not a vital few.

There are certainly other things that need to happen in order to keep our business moving forward, but the two things that only I can do that make a significant impact on our bottom line, financially and otherwise, are creating content and connecting with people.

Someone else can answer customer service e-mails, upload my blogs to my website and our e-mail service provider, edit video and audio content, run Facebook ads, design our graphics, schedule social media, manage our team, oversee day-to-day operations, track our bookkeeping, and occasionally even write some copy, but no one else can get to the essence of what I want to teach when I'm creating new content, and no one else can be me at events or online when I'm connecting with people, which is one of the things that lights me up the most too!

You'll find, as I have, that your vital few will also include the things that you love to do the most. The Universe has a divine plan, and it's organized around the fact that the things that light you up the most are also the things that allow you to have the biggest impact in the world. Isn't that just the beans?

So, when I face overwhelm and a burgeoning to-do list, which happens quite often, I nip it in the bud by getting refocused on my vital two. If my kid is sick, I don't have power and have to go search for Internet at a coffee shop, or there's some other reason that I have way less time in a given day or week, I get focused on my vital two and let the rest go. My vital two are the same as the 20 percent of my actions that create 80 percent of the results that I'm solely responsible for in our business.

If you aren't immediately able to identify the few things that you and only you can do in your career and that move the needle forward, try the exercise on the next page to identify your 20 percent items. When I did it, I was actually quite shocked by the results and was able to release a decade's worth of guilt for having "frittered my time away" during my twenties when I was living in NYC.

Step One:

Draw a line lengthwise down the center of a piece of paper.

Step Two:

On the left side, write down all of the activities/tasks that you do at work. Be as specific as possible.

Step Three:

On the right side, write down your biggest career wins to date.

Step Four:

Draw a line connecting each of your biggest career wins to the activity/task that was most responsible for it happening.

Step Five:

Circle, underline, or otherwise highlight the activities/ tasks on the left side of your paper that have been re- sponsible for your big wins. These are your 20 percent, or vital few.

If you have more than three activities/tasks on the left column responsible for your big wins, see if some of them could be considered part of the same category. For example, creating content is one of my 20 percent activities, or my vital two, but within that larger category is writing blogs, writing books, creating programs and course material, speaking, etc., so I made a bigger category of creating content to cover all of those activities.

When I did this exercise, I realized that attending events and connecting with people I felt called to connect with in a meaningful way was also a big part of my 20 percent or activities that are responsible for 80 percent of my results. It was responsible for me meeting my dear friend Meggan Watterson and then speaking at the Reveal Conference back in 2012, which led me to publishing my first book. Big win! It was also responsible for me meeting Marie Forleo, learning modern marketing, being a B-School Partner for many years, and growing an online business that I can work on from anywhere, at my own pace, around my own needs and the needs of my family. Big win!

I also realized that I'd been carrying around a load of guilt about how much time and money I'd spent networking during my twenties when I lived in NYC and was in a lot of debt and "should" have been focused exclusively on generating revenue and paying off debt.

The connections I was making were genuine. They were based on an authentic desire to build relationships with these other people who I felt connected to in some way. I didn't make coffee dates with them or attend events to meet potential business collaborators or to someday get speaking gigs and a book deal. I made the connections because they fed a part of my soul.

But now I can see how many amazing wins in business came from the time, energy, and money I invested in those relationships and continue to invest in them, so staying connected is one of my vital two, and now I don't feel guilty about it anymore. Double win!

You can absolutely apply this concept to your mothering and other areas of your life as well. What parts of mothering give you 80 percent of the results (a feeling of connection with your kids, a peaceful home environment, a feeling of satisfaction in how you're showing up as a mother, just as a few examples)? And which parts of mothering are the most draining for you but turn out to not give you that much bang for your buck anyway (sitting on five different committees, signing your kids up for three different activities each per season and then carting them around to all of them, etc.)? See what happens when you dial in the vital few that give you personally the most results in your mothering (or in your marriage or in your community or in any area of your life), and then see how it feels to let some of the other things go!

So now it's your turn.

The first step of this Do Less Experiment is to identify your vital few, or your 20 percent, which you can use the previous exercise to do.

The next step is ongoing, and that's to start to spend more and more of your time on your vital few and less and less of your time on the things that don't fall into that category.

Here are some examples of how you could do that:

- At the end of each day for a month, make a list of the activities you did that day.

- Put a star next to those that were part of your vital few and celebrate!

- For each of the activities that weren't part of your vital few, ask yourself the following:

Do I love doing this? If so, keep it. Screw results. Enjoyment is everything.

If the answer is no, move to the next question.

Does this need to be done at all? If not, stop doing that thing. Pure and simple. If so, move on to the next question.

Who else could do this? Could you get help from your kids, from your partner, from a friend or family member? Is this something you're up for hiring someone else to do or perhaps trading another skill set you have that you enjoy for this service? Some obvious examples would be cleaning your house, running errands, and maybe even cooking. At work it could be bookkeeping, data management, social media scheduling, copywriting, graphic design, marketing, or any other number of things that you find yourself doing that are not on your list of two or three vital things that you and only you can do.

I understand that hiring help may not always be an option given your financial situation. (There are always ways to get help for free, whether it's through trading services or childcare hours, having a local eight- or nine-year-old who loves kids come over to play with your younger ones [a win for both you and for their parent too!] or bringing on an intern or apprentice who will work with you for free in exchange for the experience and the wisdom you'll pass on.)

However, if your finances are your block, please dive into what I share in the experiment around asking for help and the common reasons women don't get the help they need. Sometimes it's really our bank account stopping us, but sometimes it's actually our mind. I don't know which it is for you, but if you read Experiment #6, you can figure it out.

I also understand that asking for help in general can be very difficult for women, especially when we were raised by women who prided themselves on doing it all and imprinted us with the belief that we too should do it all if we're going to be worthy women. I talk a lot more about that in the next experiment too, so keep reading if getting help tends to be a sticky wicket for you.

It is amazing how much simply being aware of your vital few helps you get really good boundaries around your time. You'll get way less decision fatigue because you'll know what does and does not belong on your schedule. Saying no becomes easier and you start to do it more gracefully and more quickly. Plus, you'll gain traction *so much faster* when you stop wasting your time either on the inconsequential or on the things that someone else is so much better suited for.

I hereby am giving you permission to move toward only working on things that you love to do and that you're exceptionally good at and that move the needle forward in your career and in your life (to the degree that your current situation allows).

While our culture likes to have us believe that there's some kind of inherent value in suffering and having to put our head down and simply grin and bear doing things we hate, there really isn't any inherent value in that. It's just exhausting and prevents us from getting the results we could be getting if we got more focused on what is and isn't a good use of our time, freeing ourselves from the tyranny of shoulds.

Listen, life has plenty of challenges that come with the territory. We don't then need to load on top of it doing work that we're not suited for, that drains us, or that is a waste of our time.

While we absolutely grow stronger through adversity, I feel like life has enough adversity already without us trying to prove our worth through doing work that is frustrating, draining, and irritating. Why not move toward making our work a source of joy and replenishment as often as possible, instead?

So, as a recap:

- Identify your vital few.

- Get them tattooed on your forearm, where you can see them at all times (or write them on a sticky note at your desk).

- Review your past three months and see how much time you're actually spending on your vital few.

- Aim toward spending 80 percent of your time on your vital few over time.

- Stay vigilant and rebuild your boundaries around your time as often as possible.

- Be amazed by how much more energy you have at work, how fast your resentments dissolve, and how much more you get done in a shorter period of time!

- And, as always, please report back on how this experiment is going for you!

experiment

5

receive help

I want my daughters to know that it takes a strong woman to know when it's time to ask for help. And it takes a strong woman to be open to *receiving* it.

Knowing when you need help, asking for it, and receiving it fully when it comes requires vulnerability. I get it. It's uncomfortable. It's not how we were raised, at least not most of us. But let's not confuse vulnerability with weakness. Oh no, they are so not the same thing.

As Brené Brown says in *Daring Greatly*: "Vulnerability sounds like truth and feels like courage. Truth and courage aren't always comfortable, but they're never weakness."

Research has shown that new mothers deal better with stress and are even able to see their babies in a more positive light when they receive support from friends and family. They have higher self-esteem, feel more confident, and are more resourceful when it comes to problem-solving around raising their baby.[1]

If you haven't experienced it yourself, you've likely had at least one friend who had a hard time emotionally adjusting to motherhood. Nine to 21 percent of women experience postpartum depression or anxiety and many more have sub-clinical levels of depression and anxiety combined with stress, low self-esteem, and a loss of confidence.

The factors that make it all worse? Minimal social support and being a single parent or having a poor relationship with their partner. And the key factor that can make significant improvements in their well-being? Peer support. Also known as *help*.[2]

Now, I will say that I was raised by a woman who, over time, had no problem getting help with typical "mother/wife" tasks because it would have simply been impossible for her to do it all with the career that she chose. She calls the way she's lived for the past 15 years or so "assisted living" because she asks for help in basically every area of her life that she doesn't absolutely love doing or that she isn't really well suited for or that she's not currently working on growing through a challenge in.

I consider my mother a very strong woman, so asking for help with life logistics is something that's always come pretty easy to me because I don't see it as a sign of weakness in the slightest. When we move outside of logistics, however, I've struggled with even knowing when I need help, let alone *receiving* it.

I'm really good at navigating things on my own, and I'm the ultimate diplomat, so there's rarely drama in my life. I know just how to respond to people so that confrontation is avoided and everything remains copacetic. I've also gotten feedback from more than one person in my life that I always seem so "together" and like I don't need any help from anyone. It's been reflected back to me that I'm an incredibly private person and that it takes a long time for me to open up and really let people in.

When I first got this feedback, I was really taken aback. I see myself as willing to tell anyone anything, to be open and real. But they weren't telling me I was fake. They were telling me that I come off as seeming so together that I have a tendency to hide my vulnerabilities.

This is the place where I feel stretched when it comes to receiving help. I don't want my emotional needs to be a burden on anyone. I don't mind saying yes when help is offered for something logistical like assisting me with the food for a party. But when it comes to dealing with something around family dynamics or self-doubt, I get scared to receive help because I'm afraid my friends or family will feel responsible for my emotional well-being or that they'll see me as having fallen apart.

I was also raised by two people who, due to their upbringing and medical training, didn't show a lot of emotional vulnerability. I didn't have a lot of modeling around what it looks like to lean on others for emotional support in a healthy, interdependent way, so leaning on friends and family when I'm struggling emotionally remains a growth edge for me.

For example, I have a dear friend, Noah, who I've known for 16 years. We've seen each other through so much, but when I'm having a tough time it still feels uncomfortable to reach out to him for help, even though I know we both consider each other family and he tells me he's there for me all the time. When I let his support in and receive the love and help he has to offer, it feels amazing, but I'm still working on making a habit out of it. The roots of my belief in the importance of seeming like I have it all together run really deep, but I'm pulling them up a little bit more every time I say yes when someone offers to be there for me.

But what I know is that this is just a blueprint. It's simply a learned habit of keeping it all together on my own so as not to become a burden to anyone. In other words, it's a learned blueprint and I'm working on unlearning it.

The other thing I know is that it's kept me separate from people. It's alienated me from true, deep connections. And, at times, it's robbed me of the sense of belonging and being held that being vulnerable creates.

So, dear one, I simply want you to know that wherever you struggle to receive help, I've been there too. And in some ways I'm still there with you.

But will you make me a promise if I promise you the same?

Let's both of us see what happens if we let go of the lie we've been told and that we've been telling ourselves—that having it all together or doing it all ourselves is what makes us valuable.

Let's replace it with shooting for genuine connection, true happiness, a full tank, the courage to be vulnerable by owning where we need support, and being willing to receive it when it shows up.

I'm in if you are.

The Pain of Going it Alone

When I think about how stubborn we can sometimes be when it comes to deflecting the help that's on offer, I remember one moment in particular when Penelope was about seven months old. Mike had gone on a five-day trip to California. Penelope had a cold and was waking up every 10 to 20 minutes crying. She wouldn't sleep unless she was physically touching my body, and I couldn't sleep if she was in bed with me. My body wouldn't allow me to let go and surrender to unconsciousness with my baby right there and my husband not home. I irrationally felt like if I let go and slept, I might not wake up if she cried and she'd be crying hysterically for hours while I was unconscious, or that she would fall out of the bed. (The fear of not hearing her cry in my sleep kept me from sleeping well from the minute she was born and wasn't healed until she was about nine months old and I'd been sleeping in the guest room downstairs with Mike bringing her to me to nurse in the middle of the night for about three months.)

I was driving home from a training event that I'd hosted for our local direct selling team members on a Saturday morning at my mom's office, alternately sobbing and screaming. Someone had innocently pulled down one of the blinds at the office, not knowing that these particular blinds were never to be touched because once they were pulled it was virtually impossible to get them re-rolled and they were really just for looks. As I ranted to my mother about the blind incident, she told me I needed to call Diane, who runs my mom's company, to call the guy to come and fix the blinds.

This was my breaking point, and I completely lost it. I was so angry. I was so overwhelmed. My baby wouldn't sleep at night. My baby wouldn't sleep during the day. She wouldn't stop scratching herself. Nothing I did would help heal her skin. I couldn't control any of it, and I was losing it. Having to make a call to apologize that someone had pulled down a window shade that was just for looks was more than I could handle.

When I called my mom back upon arriving home and I could barely speak because I was hiccuping through sobs, she realized that I was losing it.

She offered to come over and take care of Penelope for me so I could just take a nap. But I was so mad at her for having blinds that you can't pull at her office and for telling me that I needed to tell Diane about them being broken myself that I said no. And while help was exactly what I needed, it felt too hard to have her come over and for me to explain how to help me and for me to worry about her not being okay with the baby.

So even though I was at my edge of desperation, literally shaking and hiccuping with anger and exhaustion and overwhelm, I rejected her help and went home to lie in bed with my itchy, wide-awake baby and soak my pillowcase in my tears.

This was by far one of my hardest moments in mothering, yet it didn't have to be so hard. Help was on offer, yet I chose to go it alone instead and suffered more than I needed to as a result.

Getting Okay with Receiving Help

Okay, so modern feminism teaches us that the secret to getting what we want is to lean in, to be more aggressive, to be more assertive, to act more capable, to show less emotion, to never let them see us sweat, to never show our weaknesses, and to prove to everyone that we can, in fact, do it all. And that the fact that we happen to have ovaries and were designed to repopulate the planet will in no way affect our ability to essentially embody all of the qualities of a man while living in a woman's body (though often pretending we don't).

It's total bullshit.

Here's the truth: Leaning into your femininity does not mean being weak. Being feminine does not mean giving your power away. Being open to receiving support doesn't make you any less strong.

It's time for us to reprogram ourselves to own and accept that there's a new game in town and it's a feminism that owns embodying our femininity as a source of strength, not weakness.

Women have been taught that to be equal they must become like men. And men have been taught that to be good men they must be stoic, capable of anything, excellent providers, unemotional, and bionic. They must never admit weakness and do everything within their power to achieve things by themselves because life is about competition and proving your worth as higher than other people's. If you can do everything and do it well and never ask for help and do it better than other people, you've won.

So since men have been taught that this is what it means to "be a man" and women have been taught that to gain equality they must also "be a man," it's no wonder that we have trouble admitting that we need help in the first place, let alone accepting it when it comes along!

No man can do it alone.

No woman can do it alone.

And those who try end up alone, missing the entire point, which I believe is *connection.*

Do you want to be alone and exhausted or connected and energized? It's up to you.

How to Know When You Need to Receive Help

Sometimes we don't know we need help until it's too late. And that's okay, because we can ask ahead of time next time.

Right now, bring to mind, or better yet, jot down in a journal some times that you can remember recently or not so recently when you were super stressed out, had taken too much on yourself, and should have said yes to an offer for help but didn't.

Now think about the kind of situations you were in and if there are any common themes.

An example from my life was a few years ago during a big launch Mike and I were running in our business. It involved a few weeks of sending way more e-mails to our list and doing several live calls and webinars. At that time, he and I did most things in our business and we had a few freelancers who helped out with things that were totally out of our wheelhouse.

There was one particular e-mail about a call we were having that got sent with the wrong time because I'm notoriously bad with converting time zones. So we re-sent the e-mail, but because we were scrambling and doing way too many things ourselves, we screwed it up again. And so we had to send a third e-mail about the same frickin' call to finally communicate the accurate information.

It was embarrassing. It was expensive (because our e-mail autoresponder system charges us for every e-mail we send). It was a tipping point.

We'd been in this situation before, tweaking sales pages minutes before launch e-mails were scheduled to go out or having to resend e-mails because links were broken or information was inaccurate. We'd spent many late nights editing videos or programming web pages or putting together graphics, and while bootstrapping taught us a lot and we'd created a beautiful business doing almost everything ourselves, something had to change. Now we had a family and we were serving tens of thousands of people globally. It felt like our business was duct-taped together and we realized we needed to go pro.

For us, going pro meant releasing control of some of the aspects of our business and opening up to let our team step more into leadership. Essentially, we needed to be open to receiving the help that was available to us rather than continue to think that we were the only ones capable of running the show. (Our repeated mistakes were making it increasingly obvious that we were, in fact, not even that capable of running things on our own anyway!) No more screeching into launches frantic and exhausted. No more eleventh-hour panic. No more amateur hour.

Obviously, nothing is perfect and we still send the occasional e-mail with a broken link or wrong time zone. But because we were willing to give up control and ask for help, it happens way less often, and when it does, it's remedied quickly and professionally instead of with our hair on fire.

If I'm honest, I think part of the reason we waited so long to receive the kind of help we needed was because we thrived on the adrenaline caused by scrambling and doing everything ourselves. We loved the fast pace because it was exciting. But our business was maturing and we were maturing. If we really wanted to take care of our family and ourselves the way we knew we deserved, it was time to get support.

At the time I'm writing this, it's two years after the e-mail incident that was the last straw for us, and we have a world-class team running our company while we're on leave with our second baby girl. We're actually launching something right now, and I'm so hands-off I actually forgot the launch was even happening. As soon as we made the leap to get the help we needed, our revenue began to increase dramatically and so did our peace of mind. Plus, by receiving help, we get to support our own family the way we want to, and we also have the honor of significantly contributing to the livelihood of the families of the people who work for us.

Getting help is not just for you. It's for the people around you too.

Some signs you need help are:

- **Experiencing any kind of physical stress.** For me it usually shows up in my body and I can feel a tightness in my chest or my solar plexus or a lump in my throat. Tightness in general is a sign of stress for me. You might experience shortness of breath, a knot in your stomach, dizziness, or a headache. Getting ill, whether it's a simple cold or flu, or something more intense, is also a sign of physical stress. I got mastitis twice within the first three months of Penelope's life, and those were both sure signs that I needed to slow down and receive more support.

- **Getting irritable or resentful.** If you're starting to feel irritated at the people around you or resentful of them, it's a pretty good sign that you could use some help and you're not letting it in. If you're getting irritated or resentful about the tasks you're doing, even if it's not directed at anyone specifically, it's a pretty good sign you need some help.

- **Not fitting your nonnegotiables into your life.** When your basic needs for good food, movement, hydration, and sleep aren't getting met, you need help. Contrary to popular belief in our culture, being a working mom does not mean you have to be a walking zombie or a mere shell of a human being. You can thrive in your career, in your mothering, and in your relationship with your body (not to mention other areas), but only if you have support.

- **Getting cranky.** If you find yourself wearing your cranky pants six out of seven days of the week, something's gotta give, lady. You need help.

- **Feeling overwhelmed.** At work, at home, in life. If you're overwhelmed, you likely need help.

- **Not having time to do the things that are most important to you.** If you are finding that you aren't able to be present with your kids, focus on your most important activities at work, have a date night from time to time, or invest in the other activities or relationships that matter to you, you need help.

I'm sure there are a bunch of other ways to identify if you need help, but these are the primary ones that show up for the women I work with and for me. The next experiment is all about *asking* for help. So if this is a growth area for you, as it is for millions of women, I've got you. (And you can receive that.)

What to Get Help With

When I asked the women in our Origin community what they get help with, the list was far-reaching, and I loved reading the variety. It's not exhaustive, but it is extensive!

If you're someone who didn't have getting help modeled to you by your mother or other women in your life, it may not only be challenging to know when you need help, it might also be challenging to know what it's possible to get help with!

Read through the list on the next page, and see which items get you excited. If you don't already have a burning area where you need help in mind, pick one from the list that you'd like to start with, and then you can use it to practice the rest of the steps in this experiment.

Personal

- Lawn care
- Child care
- Home cleaning/ organizing
- Taking out the trash/ recycling
- Landscaping/ gardening
- Laundry (washing, folding, putting away, stain treatment, ironing/steaming)
- Cooking
- Buying and wrapping gifts
- Home repairs
- Personal training/private yoga/Pilates, etc.
- Financial planning
- Grocery shopping
- Dog walking/pet sitting
- Relationship coaching
- Therapy

Professional

- Web design/ programming
- Bookkeeping
- Accounting/tax prep
- Legal services
- Social media (strategy, scheduling, etc.)
- E-mail
- Copywriting
- Video/audio editing
- Branding
- Advertising
- Payroll/invoices
- Scheduling
- Administrative support

I'm a big believer that putting our attention on things energizes them and makes them more likely to happen. So no matter what your sweet monkey mind is telling you about getting help right now, whether it's that you don't have the money, you don't deserve it, there's no one around who would be willing to help you, or it's too hard to find someone and explain how to do things, start making a list of things you'd like to have help with in an ideal scenario.

When I first started my business and I didn't have the revenue to hire anyone to help me, I just started making a list of things I'd like to get help with as they came up. I knew I'd get a lot further making a list of desired support than sitting around lamenting the fact that I didn't have the money to get the support that I desired . . . yet!

Even now, when I make my weekly to-do list, if there's anything on there that someone else could do I make a note of it so that the number of things I'm doing gets smaller and smaller over time and it's made up mostly of only things I really love to do or that someone else truly can't do.

Allowing and Receiving

Still not sure what you could possibly receive help around?

My friend who's a master coach and spiritual guide, Laura Thompson Brady of thenourishedhome.com, has an excellent meditation for allowing and receiving. It goes like this:

Every day, your mantra is "I am allowing this day to be easy" and then you ask yourself the following questions:

1. What can I do to make this day easier?

2. What can I allow in this moment to make this day easier?

3. What can I let go of?

Give it a go and you'll be amazed by the spaciousness and support you attract by bringing these questions to the forefront every day!

How to Receive: You Are Worthy

Once you start opening your eyes to it, you'll start to see that there's help available for you *all over the darn place.*

Women who feel unworthy of getting their needs met (or even having needs in the first place) or who are cranky from years of not getting their needs met tend to be blind to the help that's all around them. They don't expect help, so they don't see help. We tend to get what we expect and we tend to get what we think we're worthy of.

If you have trouble accepting that your needs are worthy of being met, you'll have trouble attracting help and certainly trouble receiving it when it shows up. So how do you break the cycle and start feeling worthy of support so you can call it in and embrace it when it shows up?

I'd start with having a dialogue with yourself in a journal or meditation, or simply on a walk, about what makes you feel like you're not worthy of support.

How did your mother express her needs? Was it directly, passive-aggressively, or not at all?

How did you witness her getting her needs met? Through direct, kind communication, through having breakdowns, through manipulation, or some other way?

What happened in your family growing up when you asked for a need to be met or you asked for help? What kind of response did you get?

Answering these kinds of questions will start to shed some light on your blueprint around receiving support. When you start to realize that the way you feel today is rooted largely in the experience of your childhood self, you can also assure your childhood self that you're a grown-up now and that she's safe to have needs and that she can get them met.

Close your eyes and tune in to your little girl at whatever age you remember painful instances around getting your needs met. Tell her that she's safe, and you can take it from here as a grown-up. Sometimes, this can be all you need to do to make a shift and allow your adult self to run your life instead of your child self. Once you get your adult self running the show most of the time, it becomes way easier to receive help and support because you're no longer unconsciously limiting yourself with limited programming.

One of the biggest ways we block help from coming into our lives is by flat-out rejecting it when it's offered. When was the last time someone said, "Do you need help with anything?" And when was the last time you said, "Actually, I do! You could help me with _____"?

The people-pleasing do-it-alls within each of us want to reply, "Oh no! I've got it. Don't worry about it," but then we end up overwhelmed and resentful that no one's helping us. So you can simply start getting better at receiving help by saying, yes when someone offers. Even if it's hard for you to think of how they might be able to help you at first, simply practice saying yes and then start by giving them a little something they could do, like set the table if they're over at your house for dinner, or load the dishwasher.

Warning: For those control freaks among us, this may be hard. You may have a specific way you like to set the table or load the dishwasher, and they may not do it exactly the way you like it done. But this is an opportunity to surrender to the help that's available to you and enjoy the spaciousness of not doing everything yourself. You may even find that you get greater satisfaction out of receiving help than you do out of things being done your way. You never know!

Another great way to expand your capacity to receive is to fully accept compliments. Deflecting compliments is a really insidious way of devaluing yourself, and it's unfortunately common. The next time someone tells you how beautiful you look or what a great job you did during the presentation, simply smile and say, "Thank you!" Then remain silent. It will feel uncomfortable. Do it anyway. You'll want to tell them how much weight you've gained or how cheap the dress was or how nervous you were during the presentation or how you forgot an entire section. But what those things communicate is: "Actually, you're wrong. I don't look beautiful and I didn't do that well on the presentation and I don't feel worthy of your attention right now."

When you can't receive a compliment graciously, it also doesn't feel great to the compliment giver. Have you ever tried to give someone a gift who refused it? It's really frustrating and feels like your love has no place to go. When you don't have receptor sites for praise, you'll also have trouble growing receptor sites for help or getting your needs met because receiving both of these things requires feeling like you deserve them.

And one of the best ways to increase your feelings of worthiness is to actually receive the good that's coming your way. Through doing this, you prove to yourself that you actually deserve it (as opposed to when you deflect it, which sends your subconscious the affirmation that you are, in fact, not worthy).

When I first started practicing being a better receiver, I tried literally changing my body language and leaning back instead of leaning forward all the time.

I especially tried to do this when I was on dates or just with men in general. At the time, I was practicing turning up the volume on my feminine energy, and it was a really great anchor for me to feel if I was taking more of the active role or more of the receiving role.

This applies if you're in a same-sex romantic partnership, as well, because all relationships have polarity, though sometimes you'll be more in the feminine role and sometimes you'll be more in the masculine role (which, by the way, happens in opposite sex pairs too). If you're wanting to become a better receiver, this is more associated with feminine energy, so in your partnership (or when dating), leaning back is a great way to invite energy toward you instead of always proactively giving energy to the other person.

This can also be a great practice in business meetings if you always find yourself speaking first, taking control, or feeling like you have to lead or no one else will step up. Just see what happens if you practice leaning back just a little bit more than you usually might—literally leaning back with your body—to experiment with how that shifts the dynamic. You might be surprised by how your simple energetic shift invites other people to step up and do more than they might usually do.

Finally, noticing the things you're receiving on a daily basis is a wonderful way to increase your capacity to receive. Just like digesting our food in our stomach and intestines is a great way to create more space for nourishment to come in, acknowledging the things we've already received is a great way to create space to receive more.

One simple practice is to make a list of the things you received at the end of each day. It will take you about three minutes and is not a big deal but could have dramatic results. You could list out the help you received that day, any kind of support offered, the latte your friend bought you at the coffee shop, the compliment from the woman on the elevator who liked your boots, the sweet gesture of the gentleman at the post office who held the door open for you, a really great hug from your kiddo, an important insight or lesson that occurred to you or was shared with you, and really anything else that feels relevant that you received. The sheer act of noticing the good coming your way makes space for more good to come your way.

Finally, having a receiving mantra is a wonderful way to increase your capacity for receiving. "I'm a really good receiver," is a simple one to start with, but you can certainly come up with your own. I use mantras like this by repeating them when I'm brushing my teeth, driving my car, standing in line at the grocery store, or any other time I notice my mind is idle and has space to be directed to something useful. You could also write it in lipstick on your mirror or put it on a Post-it note in your car. Whatever works for you!

When you start practicing receiving, you'll not only be able to fully appreciate the help that's already available to you, you'll become a magnet for even more support. It's such a good way to do less!

Another key here is to always be filtering all of your tasks through three fundamental questions that we'll explore in more depth in Experiment #11: Streamline Your To-Do List:

- *Does this need to be done?*

- *Does this need to be done by me?*

- *Does this need to be done right now?*

When you get good at asking those questions all day long, you'll get so much more discerning about what you should spend time on and what you can get help on.

Basically, you gotta get help. We weren't meant to do life alone, and we certainly weren't meant to mother alone. And when you throw working on top of that, it's a done deal: You need help.

Your needs are worthy. You are worthy of having needs. You no longer need to prove your value through doing everything. You are valuable even when you get help—*especially* when you get help, because it means you see your worth beyond your ability to do all the things.

Choose one area of your life that feels like too much. Look around for what help might already be available to you. Let that help in. Receive it. Experience relief and spaciousness. It really can be that simple. Once you've done it, share your results with me on social media using the hashtag #DoLess so our community of women committed to having more by doing less (including me) can cheer you on!

experiment

6

ask for help

I can't figure a way that we can be happy and healthy as working women without getting help. No matter which way I think about it, there's just no way other than making sure we're supported.

Back in the day, children were raised in communities. There were lots of mothers around. There were lots of aunts around. There were lots of older kids around. There were lots of grandmothers. It wasn't just one woman trying to hold down the fort answering work e-mails on her phone with one hand while her toddler whines clinging to her leg as she stands over the stove making stir-fry for dinner (or attempting to).

There were hands. Always an extra set of hands. Always an extra lap. Always someone who hadn't been up all night who was able to be really present because their reserve tanks weren't empty. The work of raising children and keeping the home going was *shared*.

Then we switched from being a primarily agrarian society to an industrial one, and things shifted BIG-TIME. At first the men left home to work and make money and the women mostly stayed home to raise families and keep the household. And the biggest change was that the village turned into the apartment building or the suburban neighborhood or the rural home away from everything, where families were now separated by property and walls and doors that locked and everyone was now responsible for themselves and their own families instead of one another and one another's families.

Listen, I'm no history, anthropology, or sociology buff, but I know that while the shift from living in tribes to living in the nuclear family has been tremendous progress for our society in many ways, it's done a huge disservice to the way that our children are raised and to the group of people who remain the primary raisers of them: women.

I'm all about the postindustrial age and the freedoms of working wherever I want and owning my own home and being able to earn money for our family in the way that fuels my soul. And I love having my own space and solitude. I'm not signing up for living on a commune anytime soon.

That being said, there are ways that we can re-create a more tribal lifestyle, especially when we're raising children but also beyond, even in our modern world. In fact, studies show that one of the key factors in the lives of healthy centenarians are close social bonds.[1]

The expectation that some women have of themselves that they should be able to earn 50 percent or more of the household income, keep the home clean, schedule all of the kids' appointments, get food on the table, keep the children clean, safe, and loved, be a great wife who's the perfect combination of wholesome and sexy, and be cheerful while doing it all is complete insanity. All of that is just too much for one person. And I'm so over the need to prove something by showing how much we're capable of. All striving for doing it all leaves is an exhausted, albeit accomplished, woman whose own mental, physical, and emotional well-being have usually been sacrificed in order to check off all the things on the list and parade it around to show her worth.

I'll tell you what a woman who knows her worth knows how to do: *ask for help.*

She doesn't need to justify the space she takes up on planet Earth by showing how much she can do for everyone else. She doesn't need to show her mother or her mother-in-law or her best friend what she's capable of. She isn't looking for a badge of honor based on how many balls she can juggle solo.

A woman who knows her worth knows that it's not based on doing. It's based on *being.*

And asking for and being able to receive help is one of the primary ways she makes sure that she's capable of simply being. Who she is. For herself and everyone else.

And so that, my dear, is exactly what we're going to talk about next.

You Don't Have to Do It All to Have It All

Compared to some, I had a lot of support when we brought our first baby home from the hospital. My husband and I both ran our business from home, so neither of us had the pressure of an employer telling us when we had to leave our baby in child care or determining how much pay we'd get for how long. (Of course, as entrepreneurs we had to make our own financial plan for being able to take time off, because we didn't have any parental leave of any kind to fall back on.)

My husband was there with me every step of the way, and has continued to be the whole time. We're full-on dual parents, and I don't think I've ever met a more committed, all-in father than Mike. Plus, I have family close by, Mike's parents flew in from Indiana, we had tons of friends and family bringing us food, and our midwives were awesome. I also had a bevy of new mom friends I could call, text, or connect with in person on a weekly basis, and I even went to a newborn class with a group of other moms with babies between 0 to 12 weeks, every week from when Penelope was 4 to 8 weeks old. Plus, I would show up at a breastfeeding support group at our local hospital whenever I could get it together because sitting with other mothers and talking about whatever we wanted to talk about with a lactation consultant nearby to answer questions was so helpful.

And yet I cried reading about women raising children in community because with as much support as I was so blessed to have, it still felt really hard. And if I'm honest, I could have used more. I thought, however, that admitting I needed more help meant I was a bad mother.

Until I became a mother, I'd been able to overcome nearly every adversity I faced by working harder, using my intelligence, using my physical strength, or changing my perspective. But motherhood brought me to my knees with how little of it I was able to control. I'd never felt so out of control before, and, as a result, I was anxious and depressed for a good part of the first year.

We've all had moments in life and work that bring us to our knees because it's all just too much. So what's the solution?

It's asking for help. It's knowing when you even need help, and ideally figuring out how to know when you'll need help ahead of time more often so that you're facedown in a tear-soaked pillow wishing you could hit an eject button from your life less often.

It's important to mention that I'm not operating under the illusion that we can make motherhood—or womanhood, for that matter—easy. But this is one of those times that we can at least make it easier. As Adrienne Maree Brown said, "Easy is sustainable. Birds coast when they can." Let's be like the birds, shall we?

When I recently asked a group of working women about their experience with earning money versus staying home with kids, and how they feel about getting help with child care, housekeeping, or anything else, a common theme emerged: The feeling that they should just be able to "do it all" because it's their "job."

WOW. So we've created these roles of what it means to be a woman and a mother based on messages we've inherited from the men and women who've come before us, and we're living our lives to fulfill them. But I just don't think we've stopped long enough to ask where we got the idea that a woman and mother should be a certain way in the first place.

Are we not asking for help because we honestly feel really well supported already and we're good? Well, if so, awesome. But for far more women, it's more like the following:

We're not asking for help because we *should* be able to do it all. Because our mother expects us to. Because our husband expects us to. Because our mother-in-law expects us to. Because the other moms on the PTA seem to be able to do it all. Because our sister seems like she does it all. Because society told us that's what it means to be a valuable woman.

While it might feel seductive to do everything ourselves and get the momentary high of feeling like we've proven something or shown someone what we're made of, in the long run trying to do it all, whether we succeed or not, is simply lonely.

How to Ask for Help

My mantra for how to ask for help is:
Early, often, and kindly. Let's break that down, shall we?
I find that the earlier I ask for help, the better. I only realized by trial and error (mostly error) that it's better to ask for

help early than late (or never) because for so long I didn't realize I needed help until I was in the middle or about to be in the middle of something I couldn't handle myself.

For example, when we were planning our wedding it was time to work on the seating chart and despite having dreamed of doing the seating chart at my wedding ever since I was a little girl, I was feeling totally overwhelmed and couldn't figure out how to get started on it. I'd been procrastinating for weeks when it finally occurred to me to ask for some help. (The fact that it took me so long to realize that help was possible is yet one more reason this experiment is so important!)

I asked my sister to come over one Saturday afternoon and she immediately figured out a system for laying it all out. The seating chart was complete within a few hours, and the best part of it was that doing it was super fun and became a sweet memory of time spent together rather than yet another example of unnecessary stress. It's also not lost on me that because I asked for help this project took a few fun hours rather than ballooning into several days of unfun planning as it may have if I'd ended up doing it alone as I'd originally assumed I would.

As I write this, I'm planning Thanksgiving dinner for 18 people. I know from past experience how stressed out I get hosting people when I'm responsible for the food. Thanksgiving is a week and a half away, so I've asked for help early in the following ways:

- Delegating meal preparation to guests so that I'm only responsible for two items (the turkey and stuffing)

- Ordering items premade like pies from our local bakery so I don't get bogged down

- Asking specific people to be available for specific tasks the day before and the day of, like moving the furniture to accommodate our two tables, bringing tablecloths, setting the table, etc.

Rather than frantically asking for things the day before Thanksgiving or right in the middle of preparing, I'm asking well in advance so that it makes it easier for people to help. And I can rest easy knowing that almost everything is handled and that there will be plenty of hands available to take care of anything last-minute that comes up.

The next part of the how-to-ask-for-help mantra is "often."

When in doubt, ask for help. If you're not sure if you'll need help, line it up anyway! It's easier to say, "Oh, you know what? I don't actually need help like I thought," in the moment than it is to call someone frantically needing help when you realize you're in over your head.

One of the ways that Mike and I prevent as many moments as possible of needing help and not having it is by having a weekly meeting on Monday mornings when we go over our schedule. We have shared Google Calendars so he can see everything on my schedule and I can see everything on his.

One week we were looking at the calendar during our meeting and I realized that there was going to be about a 15-minute window on a Monday afternoon when Mike wouldn't be home yet and I would already have needed to leave for an appointment if I wanted to get there on time.

I could have tried to reschedule my appointment or asked Mike to leave his early or just prayed that I'd make it to mine on time despite leaving with a little bit of a time crunch, but instead I asked my mom to come over for 30 minutes to buffer the time between when I needed to leave and when Mike was expected to come home, so she could be with Penelope. It seemed kind of silly to ask her to essentially watch Penelope for 15 minutes, but it also felt really loving toward myself because it meant I wouldn't need to rush, and leaving myself enough time to get places and do things is one of my favorite new forms of self-care (even though it's requiring some new habit forming to implement because in the past I've been a perpetually five-minutes-late-and-rushing-out-the-door kind of gal).

I now have a ritual of planning out my week and marking down times for essentials like working out and writing, and then also seeing what I might need help with. When I combine that with my Monday morning meetings with Mike, I've gotten really good at spotting what I'll need help with ahead of time, and I ask . . . often. I don't ask for help as a last resort. I ask for it as a regular part of my weekly routine.

When you get in the habit of asking for help often, it really helps you get good at it. You'll be way less stressed out in general, and you'll break the programming that asking for help is a sign of weakness. Instead you'll begin to see it as an essential part of living interdependently with other humans, *and* it will help you see more opportunities to be genuinely helpful to others too!

Finally, I do my best to ask for help kindly. We all know that we'll attract more bees with honey than vinegar. This totally applies when asking for help.

I have asked for help when I'm up past my eyeballs and already overwhelmed and exhausted, and it's great that I did it, but the ask is usually on the cranky or desperate side when I needed help yesterday but I've delayed the ask. That's why the "kindly" part comes after "early" and "often." It's way easier to kindly ask for help when you're doing it ahead of time and when it's part of your regular MO. You've now moved from being reactive to proactive, and it's simply easier to be kind when you're calm and your central nervous system isn't in fight or flight (sympathetic) but is instead in rest and restore (parasympathetic).

Asking for help doesn't only include things like asking for dinner to be made, the trash to be taken out, or someone to help you with filing. It also includes simply knowing how to ask for your needs to be met. There are so many areas where we can ask for help once we've given ourselves permission to put down the superhero cape and welcome the experience of support.

Appreciation

When it comes to asking for help or speaking up for your needs, coming from a place of appreciation is so key.

Why? Well, think about it. Are you more likely to want to support someone who's cranky and already disappointed in you or someone who's in pure appreciation of you and radiating love toward you?

It feels good to help someone who is already in a place of appreciation. So, as women, we need to find ways to move into appreciation more often so that we become easier to help.

What's so magical about appreciation is that the more you practice it, the easier it gets. And the more you practice noticing things that you appreciate, the more things you appreciate there are to notice.

What we appreciate appreciates.

When it comes to your partner or spouse, it's absolutely miraculous to witness how the more you focus on the qualities they possess that you love, the more those qualities seem to come forward and the less you even notice the things that bug you about them. Sometimes the things that bug you about them actually disappear. Is it because they changed or because your perception changed? I don't know, but does it really matter? The result is the same.

We all know this with our kids too. When we focus on and acknowledge them for the behavior that we want to see more of, we tend to see more of that behavior versus harping on them for the behavior that we'd prefer not to see.

In fact, many proponents of the study of positive psychology talk about how our subconscious mind cannot understand the word *don't*, so when interacting with children it's much more impactful to say, "Walk by my side so I can keep you safe," than it is to say, "Don't run ahead of me" when walking on a crowded street, for example.

Putting our attention on what we want rather than what we don't want is not only incredibly powerful from a manifesting and law of attraction standpoint, it's also incredibly powerful when making requests of others in our lives.

It's not just kids, obviously, that have the tendency to ignore the word *don't* and focus only on what you said not to do. If you say, "Don't hit your sister," a kid focuses on hitting his sister. If you say, "Don't text while talking to me," your spouse's mind focuses on "text while talking to me."

It takes a little discipline but can actually become a fun practice to phrase your requests of not only your children, your partner, and your co-workers in the positive, but also your requests of the Universe.

So give it a go. Ask for help. Then give me a shout on social media using the hashtag #DoLess to let me know how it went. Be ready for your life to be revolutionized by this simple yet powerful step!

experiment

7

simplify

Doing things the simplest way is not my default. I have a tendency to overcomplicate things and do more if I allow my default settings to take over. But what happens when I do that is that I get overwhelmed and cranky and I wish I hadn't made things so complicated.

My last book launch was a perfect example. In addition to two book launch parties (one in my hometown of Portland, Maine, and one in NYC) and the media that Hay House had lined up for me, I decided to pitch a bajillion podcasts and host my own interview series of 50 people telling their own Money Love Stories.

We started a hard-core prelaunch in August, and by October I had to be peeled off the floor with a spatula. I had definitely done too much. And while the book launch was absolutely a great success, I don't think it required as many elements in order for it to be as successful as it was.

Looking back, what I would have done differently is focus on a few key elements that really move the needle on getting the word out as opposed to doing tons of things, some of which made a huge difference and some of which didn't.

Life is like this. We wake up one day and realize our lives are really full and we're exhausted and wondering: Is this all there is?

Despite what our commercial culture would have us believe, the answer to this feeling of tired emptiness is not to add more to our lives, though. The answer is to strip back what's not adding to our satisfaction and joy so we're left with the simple basics of what really matters.

In Experiment #2, we talked about what really matters to us, and now I want to take it even deeper. Let's dig into the question: How do I actually simplify my life so that I feel more satisfied and less tired?

A group of ladies from our Origin community told me how they reprioritized their lives to free up more resources for getting help and other things they wanted.

I loved their ingenuity and resourcefulness:

One woman in our community, Ruth, went over her bills with a fine-toothed comb and realized through asking for late fees to be reversed, noticing things she was getting charged for that she wasn't using, canceling recurring payments for things she no longer wanted, and shopping around for lower rates on things like her Internet and car insurance, she was able to save over $100 per month. Think about what you could do with an extra $1,200 a year that might be getting squandered away on things you don't even want.

(Mike and I did something similar a year ago when we changed health insurance, saving us $300 per month, and then sold his car and leased a new one, saving us another $200 per month. $500 per month saved equaled $6,000 a year that we could redirect toward getting more support in our business!)

Streamlining our finances is a beautiful place to start simplifying. Another mother in our community, Beth, started selling things in mom buy-and-sell groups online that she would have previously donated. She also started refinishing and selling furniture she found for free at the end of people's driveways. She also started cooking more vegetarian meals, subbing beans for meat, and eating out less. Hello, found money that could be redirected toward support! Way to simplify and, as a result, find more resources.

Sarah shared that she and her husband went from two dressers to one, each cutting their wardrobe in half so that they share one dresser and one closet. She now only buys clothing quarterly, if at all, and she loves having a few core outfits and not having any wasted time, money, or energy around getting dressed.

Sylvia signed up for a meal delivery service called Home Chef where recipes and ingredients are delivered to her. Then, she and her son get to have fun making the food together. They also got an organic lawn-care service and a cleaning service for her home (annual windows and carpets included) to optimize the time she has to spend with her son and her husband. They canceled their cable and unlimited data on their phones, and stopped buying brand-new cars in order to redirect their spending so they could have more of what they truly value: time with each other. Automating things like getting their dinner ingredients delivered to their home (plus having meals planned for them ahead of time) and cleaning has created much more simplicity for this working mother so she can save her brain space for the higher-leverage stuff.

Mary shared that her husband makes most of their furniture, or she finds exactly what she wants discarded by other families. They've chosen to live in a smaller house so that they can live on one income and she can be home with her kids and not feel pressured to bring in money (though she does have a business as an artist and creative coach).

What I love about all of these examples is that all of these women looked at ways that doing more, spending more, and having more were costing them the ability to have what they really wanted. So they looked at where they would be willing to simplify or live outside the box in terms of what's expected of us in society so that they could have what really mattered to them: money to spend on things they valued, child care so they could take care of themselves, more time with their children without financial pressure, etc.

Why Simplify?

Adding more to our lives complicates them. Complications lead to logistical wrangling that takes a lot of time and energy that then can't be invested in the things that lead to the most joy and satisfaction.

I know a family who manages four different homes. They use three of them nearly every single week, and between all of the time they spend thinking about which of their things are where and handling the logistics of keeping the homes clean and maintained, not to mention shuttling back and forth, they've basically spent their entire week.

I recently heard of a woman who has three kids, ages five, three, and one, who has her own consulting business and also sits on the board of trustees for her college, which is two and a half hours north of where she lives. She finds herself needing to do that drive every two weeks or so to sit on one subcommittee or another, and between the kids, her business, and the board, the logistics are freaking complicated.

The reason to simplify is, simply, to make your life easier. The less your life is bulging at the seams with complexity, the more space you have to show up for what truly matters.

The Culprits

Here are the things I can think of that add the most complexity to my life (or have in the past) and the lives of those around me:

- Belongings: clothing, furniture, cars, boats, kitchen gadgets, and basically anything and everything that requires maintenance, cleaning, organization, and storage
- Meetings
- Trying to make other people happy
- Overthinking things
- Multiple residences
- Travel
- Feeding yourself and your family
- Taking on responsibilities beyond your fundamental needs and those of your family
- Moving
- Multiple jobs or businesses
- Activities
- Relationships
- Saying yes to too many things
- Living according to other people's expectations
- Not having good boundaries
- Working on multiple projects at the same time
- Trying to do everything yourself

How Do We Simplify?

Again, as a default I will always resort to more. Simplicity is not my automatic urge, so I've had to develop a skill for simplification over time.

When we look at a business project, for example, our entire company has what we call the "Do Less Filter," which everything has to go through. If there's a way that we could get as good results in a less complex way, in a way that requires fewer steps, or doing less in general, we do it.

Why? Saved time. Saved energy. More space. More ease.

The "Do Less Filter" has become a way of life for me, and it's become a key path to simplicity for this lady who has a tendency to overcomplicate things. It's been a lifesaver, honestly.

The key question to ask yourself when it comes to absolutely any area of your life is this:

Is there a way I could get the desired result here with fewer action steps or fewer elements or in less time?

Your desired outcome might be a revenue goal in your business, a sales target at work, a way you want to feel in your marriage, or a desire you have around your relationship with your kids. It doesn't matter. The same question applies.

If you start asking yourself this question on a regular basis, you'll realize how much time and energy you've previously wasted making things more complicated than they need to be.

Now, there might be a circumstance where you get a ton of joy out of a set of meticulous steps to get a desired outcome, like baking homemade bread and then making stuffing out of it from scratch for your family's Thanksgiving. Is it more complicated than buying the bread and then making the stuffing? Yes. But the joy you get from the process outweighs the fact that it's more complicated.

I'm talking more about things like packing up all of your stuff without going through it first and putting it in storage for a year while you travel, only to come home to a higher than necessary storage bill that's half full of things you could have gotten rid of a year ago and not needed to move twice.

I find that I tend to make things more complicated than they need to be when I'm rushing. I get stuck in a constant complication cycle because the more complicated things become, the more time they take me and the more stressed out I become, thus leaving me not enough time to take the space I need to step back and actually see that I've overcomplicated things. Plus, when I'm stressed out I don't have the mental clarity to see how things could be simpler.

The other thing that can stop overcomplicating things in its tracks is meditation. Now, I must be honest, I'm more of an aspiring meditator than an actual meditator in terms of sitting down daily with my eyes closed and breathing for a set period of time. That being said, throughout the day I do close my eyes and take a few breaths whenever I feel like I need a reset, and just this alone can stop my head swirling long enough to see things from a new perspective and allow me to see a simpler solution than I could have if I had just plowed on through without pausing to breathe and feel. (If you want a great place to start or to simplify your meditation practice, check out my friend Rebekah Borucki's book, *You Have 4 Minutes to Change Your Life.*)

Ideas for Simplification

Here is a list of crowdsourced ideas for simplifying your life as a working mother that I got from our Origin community:

- diaper delivery service

- meal planning/ingredient delivery service

- batching tasks/time blocking things like errands, content creation, writing, making phone calls, housework, etc., so that time isn't wasted on jumping from task to task and getting distracted

- grocery delivery

- keeping kids' toys to a minimum

- saying good-bye to relationships that add unnecessary complications

- cutting back on your children's activities (one friend of mine has a one-activity-per-season-per-kid rule)

- paring down your wardrobe to only things you love that work really well together (aka a capsule wardrobe)

- making most of your meals out of just a few ingredients and keeping your meal rotation minimal to save time, energy, and money

- not exchanging holiday gifts, or cutting down on how many or with whom you exchange

- keeping only one bag, one backpack, and one mini purse to prevent things getting lost in different bags

- not owning high heels and only owning one other pair of shoes per season plus sneakers, rain boots, and flip-flops

- getting rid of extra cars

- working from home so there's no commute

- agreeing on who does what chores around the house so it's preset and doesn't need to become an issue or struggle
- laundry pickup/delivery
- donating things rather than going through the hassle of trying to sell them

For this Do Less Experiment, first identify which area of your life feels the most complicated or which aspect of your life feels like it complicates your life the most.

Can you pinpoint what exactly it is about that aspect of your life that's complicated?

What's one thing you could do to simplify it?

Use the list above as inspiration and try one of those things or come up with your own!

Living simply doesn't necessarily mean living like a minimalist (though it can if that appeals to you!). I by no means consider myself a minimalist (my husband and I have an ongoing joke about the number of throw pillows in our house that simply bring me a lot of joy from their beauty), but I continue to aim toward simplicity.

When you make steering toward simplicity an ongoing focus, you'll find that your life becomes more effortless. When your life is simple, doing less actually becomes the default, and it's a really beautiful thing.

8

manage your energy

I became obsessed with the elusive promise of balance, enough time for everything, and feeling in control of my life that time management offers at the young age of 14, when I got my first Day-Timer.

In college, I would write out everything that I was going to do in my day into timed blocks, including eating and showering, and attempt to follow my rigid plans so that I would somehow fit it all in. (I never did manage to "fit it all in," for the record.)

Anyone else who, like me, has tried every planner on the market and read every time management book out there and tried all of the systems knows, though, that no matter how well you schedule your time in theory, you still never feel like you got it all done.

Since becoming a mother, I've learned to really shift my expectations and focus from checking items off my to-do list to having enough energy to be present for the things that really matter to me. This shift has been pivotal in my level of sanity and happiness.

As a result of realizing my satisfaction came from being more present instead of doing more tasks, I started focusing on managing my energy instead of my time. Why? Because according to Einstein's theory of relativity, the perception of time is dependent on the mass and speed of the object relative to which the speed of light is being measured.

If you, like me, are not a physicist, here's a more practical way of explaining it that relates more to our everyday lives, where we're probably not measuring the speed of light:

Our experience of time is relative. Relative to what, though—that is the question.

Well, the ancient Greeks knew what was up. They had two different names for time. *Chronos* describes linear time that passes by at a set speed in set increments and that we only have so much of. *Chiros,* on the other hand, describes time that suspends or speeds up depending on what's happening as that time is passing.

We've all had experiences of the difference between chiros and chronos in our lives. The five minutes you stood in line at the coffee shop this morning waiting for your latte felt really different from the five minutes you spent holding your child for the first time after birth.

The difference in how we experience time is our energy . . . essentially how present we are or how we are interacting with time passing.

Mihaly Csikszentmihalyi wrote about the experience of flow in his book by the same name, or the state of the perfect cocktail of taking joy in an action while also being fully engaged and challenged enough by it that we're totally present. When we're in states of flow, we don't think about time. We're experiencing chiros, or timelessness.

What I've found is that when I focus on managing my energy instead of managing my time, I end up having enough time for the things that really matter to me. I care less about getting all of the other things done because I'm so present in my life that I feel fulfilled without needing to tie my worth to checking things off my to-do list.

So how do we manage our energy?

The first thing to do is to look at where your energy is leaking the most. As a working mother, you may feel like you have a limited amount of energy and that it's totally spent at the end of the day.

But it doesn't have to feel that way.

Usually, there are one or two key culprits for energy drainage in our life, and when we figure out how to plug those up, all of the other areas of our life improve dramatically as well. The different areas of your life are not silos. They're all interconnected, and as much as the patriarchal working world would have us compartmentalize everything and pretend that all the parts of our life don't affect one another, they do. We're integrated. We just are.

To start off with, here are the main areas of your life that might be the primary energy drains. Read through them and see which one feels like it's probably the main culprit:

- Your mothering

- Your career

- Your romantic relationship(s)

- Your nuclear family

- Your extended family

- Your friendships

- Your health

- Your spirituality

- Your finances

Once you've identified which of those is draining the most of your energy, then it's time to dig in a little deeper about what in particular is so draining about that particular area. For example:

- If it's your mothering, is it that you feel guilty about not spending enough time with your kids or not being present enough while you're with them?

- If it's your career, is it that you find your boss nearly intolerable in the way she interacts with you and your co-workers?

- If it's your romantic relationships, is it that your partner just seems unhappy and doesn't appear to want to get out of his or her funk?

- If it's your extended family, is it that you feel like your mother is too needy with you and depends on you to get her emotional needs met?

Whatever pops into your head first is probably what it is. You don't need to edit yourself here. Go with your gut. No one else has to read your mind and find out that you think they're your primary energy drain. This is not information for public consumption.

The good news is that the simple act of becoming aware of a particular area of your life that's really draining your energy is often enough to shift things. You may change your behavior, perception of, or the dynamic around that area of your life without even trying to now that you know it's sucking you dry energetically.

But it never hurts to add a little fuel to the cleansing fire, so now is a good time to identify what one simple action step is that could help to plug the energy leak.

Again, the first instinct is usually the best here.
If you feel stuck, here are some examples:

- If you're feeling drained by feeling guilty about not being present with your kids, you could implement a rule for yourself where for the first 20 minutes after they come home from day care or school you put down whatever you're working on (including your phone) and are totally present with them, whether it's playing, having a snack, or simply listening to them talk about their day.

- If it's your intolerable boss, you could look at what her behavior triggers in you from your past to see if identifying the trigger makes her less irritating to be around. You could also give some compassionate feedback or begin looking for another job.

- If it's your partner seeming unhappy and unwilling to do anything about it, you could create a new habit where you try to do something that improves your own happiness, like take a walk outside, try a new recipe, or watch one of your favorite TV shows.

- And if it's your emotionally needy mother, you could set a boundary with her where you tell her you love her and that she needs to find another outlet to get her emotional needs met in addition to her relationship with you.

Now, I'm not saying that plugging your energy leak will necessarily be easy. But it will be WELL WORTH IT because the energy you save from not losing it out a black hole of your life will infinitely uplift every other area of your life.

Setting that boundary with your mother will make you feel suddenly energetic and willing enough to get back to your weekly workouts.

Investing in your own happiness instead of pouring all of your lifeblood into your partner will give you the pep in your step to start the novel you've always dreamed of writing.

Finally doing something about feeling guilty for not being present with your kiddos will give you the energy to do meal preparation on Sunday nights like you've been meaning to do but feeling too tired to do.

And you know what? Investing your energy in areas that really uplift you instead of drain you is even more energizing. When you begin to see your energy as the precious resource it is, you get way more done in less time, you're better able to see what's a priority and say no to what's not, and you get on this beautiful upward spiral where getting more energized simply leads to feeling more energized and so on!

Aligning with Cycles

I've also found that aligning my activities and the focus of my weeks with the phases of my cycle or the phases of the moon if I'm not cycling has been miraculous in terms of giving me enough energy for everything.

As we talked about earlier, women are cyclical creatures, and when we start working with our cycles instead of fighting them, we tap into our superpowers of manifestation and creation.

Our bodies are so wise. Every different kind of task you might need to do will fit into one of the four phases of your menstrual cycle or the coinciding cycle of the moon, and when you begin to align your schedule with your cycles, you'll find that you have more energy for the task at hand when you're doing it *at the right time of your cycle.*

Now, this does not mean that 100 percent of your activities will be scheduled during the appropriate phase. Life doesn't work that way. There are way too many variables, unknowns, and unexpected things that come up.

But if you can try to do even 10 to 20 percent of the ideal activities within the optimum phase for those activities, you'll be amazed by the kind of momentum you create and by how replenished you begin to feel, as opposed to feeling drained.

As a quick review, here are the phases of your menstrual cycle with the coinciding lunar phase, to use if you're not cycling, with the kind of activities that are ideal for that phase:

- Follicular/waxing crescent: Starting things, brainstorming, planning

- Ovulation/full moon: Connecting, getting out there, collaboration, communication

- Luteal/waning crescent: Detail-oriented work, bringing projects to completion, tying up loose ends

- Menstrual/new moon: Rest, evaluation, and research

The simple act of tracking your cycle and the moon, like we did in Experiment #1, will do wonders for your ability to have more energy, because you won't be wasting energy beating yourself up for feeling the way you feel when it's completely natural to feel that way during the particular phase of your cycle.

I continue to be shocked by the amount of time women spend beating themselves up for feeling more inward for half of the month. Our culture has told us that we're supposed to be "on and out" all month because it celebrates the traits of the masculine over the feminine and being outward is a masculine trait. (Remember, this is not about male or female. For example, I'm a woman who has more of a tendency toward being "on and out." So that particular masculine trait is very strong in me.)

But the luteal and menstrual phases of our cycle (or the waning phase of the lunar cycle between the full moon and the new moon) which is a full half of the month are a more inward time. And that inward time is hugely valuable! It's where we can get so much traction in completing projects and gain important insights from a combination of our logical and intuitive minds, when our brain is the most wired for connecting both hemispheres during our menstrual phase.

Imagine that you have a project at work that is going to require some brainstorming and planning, some collaboration with other team members, some sitting down and doing the work of getting things on paper and actually putting the ideas into a form that is useful for your company. Before this project moves on to the next phase, it also will require some research.

Wouldn't it be magical if instead of trying to push through what you're currently feeling emotionally or physically, you actually honored where your energy is and did the different parts of the project at the different times of your cycle over 28 days that would make you poised to capitalize on the kind of energy that your body or the cosmos is experiencing at that time?

Partnering with your body and the cosmos in terms of what phase of your cyclical nature you're currently in is one of the smartest ways to do less, yet have more . . . and certainly one of the smartest ways to experience enough energy for everything.

(Remember that you can use the Daily Energy Tracker, which can be found in Appendix A, to help you work with your cycles and the moon's cycles.)

When you track your own experience of the different days of your cycle and different phases of your cycle (or the moon), over time you start to get really good data on how you feel at different times of your 28 day-ish rotation.

If you look back over three months of Daily Energy Tracker data and find, for example, that on day 20 of your cycle you always feel like being alone and doing work that doesn't require you to talk to anyone, instead of scheduling meetings and outings on day 20, you can always set yourself up for success by making that a solo workday.

When you get to know your own energetic patterns intimately, you can then begin to design your life around them and also let the key people in your life know about them so they can be helpful as well.

Reduce Draining Relationships

There are people who are energizing, and there are people who are draining. And sometimes people who you used to find energizing now drain you. It doesn't mean they're bad. It doesn't mean you're bad. It just means the relationship isn't serving you anymore or that the way you're engaging in the relationship isn't serving you.

If you want to have more energy for the things that truly matter in your life, you have to stop donating it to people who are using it as their life force. They need to figure out how to cultivate their own life force and stop siphoning yours.

I understand that letting a relationship go is easier said than done, and sometimes it seems impossible, especially when the one draining your energy is your mother or the person you married! The good news is, while sometimes you do actually need to end relationships, sometimes all you have to do is change the dynamic to stop the energy suckage.

I'm not a psychologist, nor do I play one on TV, but I do know that when you're in an energetic dance with someone and you have a certain dynamic, as soon as you change the way you're behaving, they can no longer do the same dance either. They have to change their dance.

How do you know which people in your life are draining your energy? Well, it's the people that, after you spend time with them, you feel drained. Pretty simple to spot.

As you read this, I'm sure there's one key person who comes to mind who's the primary energy sucker in your life. Give your relationship a little thought right now, and if you want extra credit, grab a journal and do some writing about it.

Ask yourself:

What is it about this person exactly that drains me? What specific behavior do I find sucks my energy?

What part do I have in the dance that keeps this particular dynamic in place?

How could I change my part of the dance so that they also shift?

I was friends with a woman who always had a lot of drama going on. She was vivacious, really fun, hilarious, and creative, and sometimes I loved hanging out with her. But there was often some kind of dramatic situation that she would have emotional breakdowns about and I would find myself playing therapist. Each situation seemed to come up over and over and over again and would take a really long time to get resolved.

I valued our friendship, and I didn't want to just end it, so instead of "breaking up" with her because I was starting to feel tired every time we hung out, I decided to simply change the dance I was doing.

The next time she launched into the drama of the day and started becoming emotionally unhinged, I imagined buttoning up my energy field so that I was protected from her leaky energy. I listened while maintaining my invisible emotional boundary and then I responded that I was so sorry she was going through this.

What came next was so key. Instead of commiserating with her about how awful it was or leaping in to try and save her and fix the problem, I simply asked her what she thought she was going to do about it.

It was like she had been handing me a bowl of turds every time we got together all of these months and this time instead of holding the bowl for her I simply handed it right back. The dynamic shifted instantly, and before I knew it she was off the drama topic and on to something way more fun and energizing. From then on out, our whole relationship shifted and we were able to simply appreciate being in each other's company rather than playing into the dynamic where she fell apart and I tried to put her back together.

Hallelujah! Energy hole plugged. This works with family members too, by the way.

Now, I've also had relationships where they simply had to end. Changing my end of the dance wouldn't have been enough. Sometimes these relationships fizzle over time (that's been my experience more often than not), and sometimes they require a direct, loving conversation. Either way, it will be well worth the extra energy you feel when that person is no longer feeding off of you.

Last, there are people who drain you who you can't end the relationship with because they're family or they're your next-door neighbor or your child's best friend's mother or something like that.

First, try changing your side of the relationship dance.

Second, imagine an energetic bubble around yourself when you're with them, to protect yourself from their siphoning. (This can literally be as simple as closing your eyes and taking a deep breath when you're in the car about to see them and visualizing an egg or bubble around you that protects you and then getting out of the car and going to see them. No need to overcomplicate it.)

Third, reduce the amount of time you spend with them. If you can't eliminate time spent, reduce it as much as possible and add in buffers (like other people who defuse the situation or activities that pull the focus off the relationship) to keep you energetically safer.

If energy suckers are a huge issue in your life, I also recommend checking out my mom's book on this topic, *Dodging Energy Vampires*. Interpersonal relationships also tend to be the stickiest wickets for all of us, so please call upon a professional, like a therapist or really great coach, to help you with these energy-sucking relationships if you feel like you need extra aid. I've gotten great support in this area of my life from a number of trained professionals who've saved me years of grief and drama.

Remember: Showing vulnerability and asking for help is not weakness. It's a sign of tremendous strength and self-love.

Bringing It Back

So, as a review, to practice conservation of energy in your own life, you'll want to:

- Identify the top area of energy leakage in your life.

- Come up with a way to stop some of the energy leakage.

- Start syncing your activities with the phase of your menstrual cycle or the lunar cycle to the best of your ability (knowing that 10 to 20 percent is amazing).

- Identify the biggest energy drainers in your life.

- Change your dance with them.

- Reduce time with them or eliminate time with them, as necessary.

Once you've started managing your energy, start to notice how your relationship with time shifts. You'll be amazed by how different time feels (and how much more of it you have) when you have your energy back!

experiment

9

make sleep
a spiritual practice

I never understood how tired it was possible to feel until having kids. Our first daughter didn't sleep through the night consistently until she was almost two, and our second didn't come out of the womb totally competent in the sleep department either.

I turn into a pumpkin at about 10 P.M. Most nights these days I'm in bed by 9 P.M. and lights are out by 9:30 P.M. Sleep is a nonnegotiable, and there's a minuscule list of things that could inspire me to lose my precious sleep. The only thing I can think of right now is taking a red-eye so I don't have to miss being with my family for an extra day when I'm traveling without them. Other than that, sleep is *it*.

More and more research is coming out about the importance of healthy sleep. Thanks to Arianna Huffington and some other sleep crusaders, our cultural perception of sleep is changing, and it's about time. It's becoming less common to wear how little we slept as a badge of honor and try to make do on as little as possible.

There are simply certain times during motherhood when sleep is outside our control. When Penelope was less than six weeks old, our midwives came by for a home visit and asked me how sleep was going. I told them that she was sleeping at night for one- to two-hour stretches and I was waking and nursing her for about 45 to 60 minutes with each waking. (P had a tough time latching for a while, so nursing was less than efficient. Plus, I wasn't a huge producer, so each session required both sides before she was ready to go back to sleep.)

They told me how important it was for my recovery after labor and the C-section to be getting a minimum of four hours of sleep in a row each day, and I was like, "Well, thank you for that information. How the hell am I supposed to get four hours of sleep in a row when my kid is up every one to two hours needing to nurse, especially when you're telling me how important it is for her to eat because she's still not back to her birth weight?"

I know they meant well, but it was soooo not helpful advice right in that moment.

So, lest I too become sooooo not helpful to your already strung-out and exhausted self, who's doing everything within her power to get sleep but is being thwarted by tiny humans screaming, poking at you, or otherwise simply not allowing you to sleep, I give you permission to skip this experiment, because I certainly don't want to add insult to injury here.

(Before you go to the next experiment, just read the section in this one on yoga nidra, because it's kind of like this hidden secret to getting the benefits of restful sleep in 20 minutes. It's like sleep hacking, and if you're totally sleep deprived, it may totally save your life.)

If, on the other hand, you've got a sleeper and you feel like the amount of sleep you're getting each day is somewhat within your control, then this experiment is for you. And if you're someone who currently, or has ever, gotten off on their ability to function on less than seven hours of sleep a night and is currently, or has ever in the past been, proud of your lack of sleep, then you *definitely* need to read this experiment. It might be the most important one for you in the book.

Sleep Is Not a Waste of Time

When I was growing up and my sister and I were in our teens, she would often sleep until noon or later on the weekends. My dad would be all worried about it and would talk about how she was "wasting the day." The message was: Sleep isn't valuable. Only doing things is valuable. Sleep isn't doing anything. You should feel guilty for sleeping.

But the truth is she was an adolescent girl who, even now, still has a tendency to be a night owl and she needed rest. There were so many hormonal changes going on in her body, so many emotional shifts, and so much growth and reorganization overall. Sleep was deeply restorative for her and incredibly productive for her system. (On average, adolescents need 9 ¼ hours of sleep a night, and they actually tend toward going to sleep later and waking later during this time in their lives.)[1]

When we sleep, there are so many crucial processes going on that cannot happen when we're awake. It's the ultimate practice in doing less to have more. Very similar to the way your body makes an entire human without you even thinking about it while you're pregnant, your body does profound repair and restoration without you even thinking about it *while you're unconscious.*

In case you've forgotten, our bodies are miraculous. Here are just a few of the things that happen while we sleep, according to howsleepworks.com:

- Our long-term memory gets organized.
- We integrate new information.
- Neurotoxins get neutralized.
- Cells get repaired.
- Physical wounds are healed (the process is expedited through sleep).
- The immune system is strengthened.
- Growth hormone increases, which is important for tissue regeneration and repair.
- Muscles grow.
- Hormones are synthesized.

Lack of sleep will eventually make you psychotic[2] and can actually kill you.[3] That's why sleep deprivation is used as a form of torture. (Hello, first year of motherhood! No wonder it's such a gauntlet for so many of us!)

Let's assume that you're not so sleep deprived that you've gone psychotic, and you're reading this, so lack of sleep hasn't killed you. But you may be interested to know that sleep deprivation has been linked with the following less-than-ideal outcomes:[4]

- Increased risk of obesity
- Overeating
- Increased risk of some cancers such as colorectal and breast cancer
- Increased risk of diabetes

- Increased likelihood of an accident
- Increased likelihood of catching a cold
- Loss of brain tissue
- Loss of focus
- Memory loss
- Increased likelihood of being emotionally reactive and unable to produce appropriate responses
- Increased risk of death
- Decrease in sperm count (good to know for the men in our lives)
- Increased risk of heart disease
- Four times the risk of stroke
- Decrease in attractiveness and approachability
- Increase in skin aging

If you read that whole list and still feel like sleep is a waste of time, you're probably sleep deprived and not computing information very well. I'd recommend a nap and getting to bed early.

According to the National Sleep Foundation, adults 18 to 65 years old need 7 to 9 hours of sleep a night to function optimally. Infants need 12 to 15, toddlers need 11 to 14, preschoolers need 10 to 13, school-age children need 9 to 11, and teens need 8 to 10. After 65 years old, 7 to 8 hours a night are recommended.

I'm one of those people who does really great on 9 to 10 hours of sleep a night. My husband, Mike, does surprisingly well on 6 to 7 hours a night. So all of this is on a spectrum, of course, and you have to know your own body.

Does It Matter When You Go to Bed?

Your sleep happens in 90-minute cycles during which your brain moves from non-REM (rapid eye movement) sleep to REM sleep. Non-REM sleep is said to be deeper and more restorative than REM sleep.

As it gets closer to dawn, we spend more time in REM sleep than in non-REM sleep, so getting to bed between 8 P.M. and 12 A.M. will increase the amount of more restorative, non-REM sleep that you get. Dr. Allison Siebern, associate director of the Insomnia & Behavioral Sleep Medicine Program at Stanford University, says that the best time to go to sleep is when you're the most tired. (Don't you love it when science confirms common sense?) She says if you're a night owl and going to bed at 9 P.M. feels painfully early, wait until you're more tired. And if you're a morning person and staying up past 10 P.M. feels like torture (raising my hand), then go to bed earlier.[5]

The key here: listen to your body. But know that if you have a tendency to go to bed really late (after midnight), you might want to experiment with an earlier bedtime and see if that makes you feel happier, more clear minded, and better able to manage your life.

Yoga Nidra: The Ultimate Sleep Hack

My friend Sarah introduced me to yoga nidra, also known as yogic sleep, a form of meditation, when I was struggling with postpartum insomnia and the very unique torture of not being able to sleep when my newborn was finally asleep. (It's like being famished and sitting behind a glass window, on the other side of which is a steaming, delicious feast that you're incredibly close to but yet still cannot reach.)

I bought the CDs of the guided practice but never did them. Then, out of the blue a woman named Karen Brody, a playwright whose play *Birth* I was already familiar with, joined Mike's and my direct sales team, the Freedom Family. It turns out her most current work was focused on leading a rest revolution, and at the center of it was none other than yoga nidra. I tried it once at the end of a teleconference with her, but found doing it on the phone distracting, and I couldn't quite let it sink in.

The third tap on the shoulder from the Universe came when I was teaching at Wanderlust, a yoga and music festival, and I found myself completely exhausted one afternoon. I dragged my butt to a yoga nidra class with two of my girlfriends with minimal expectations of what the 30-minute experience might hold for me.

What happened was miraculous. After less than a minute in the darkened room, lying on my back supported by pillows, I was transported by the angelic voice of the teacher, Tracee Stanley, and I found myself in an altered state.

I could hear her voice, and I was definitely conscious, but I felt like I'd gone into a deeper state of stillness and calm than I'd experienced in a long time. I was aware that Tracee was speaking, but I wasn't tracking every single word like I would have been if she and I were chatting over a cup of tea.

My body felt heavy yet suspended all at once. I felt like I'd traveled to another planet, a planet where there was nothing to worry about, where I was completely held, where I was enough, and nothing other than breathing (which I didn't even have to think about) was necessary. It was Planet Rest, and I loved it there.

When the meditation was over, I felt like I'd taken a three-hour nap. I felt mental clarity, physical energy, and a sense of bliss like I've only felt after really amazing sex or rare moments of profoundly deep meditation. I later read in Karen's book *Daring to Rest* that yoga nidra helps you access a deeper level of rest than even sleep often does, therefore allowing you to rest on a deeper level than you're likely used to.

Obviously exhaustion in women is an epidemic, yet so many of the women who need rest the most, mothers, simply can't get the rest that they need. But they could find 15 minutes to do yoga nidra. And what's so cool is that once you access the depth of rest that yoga nidra offers, you will find yourself feeling more rejuvenated by the sleep you can get, even if it's not as much as you'd like.

Karen says that yoga nidra, beyond helping you rest, accesses your subconscious mind and helps you step fully into your purpose and power. That makes sense because when we're exhausted we're just barely keeping it together, unable to find the energy to be powerful or purposeful, but when our tank is full we're unstoppable.

Sleep Heals Everything

When my heart was broken, I found that sleep sped up the mending. When I have a cold or the flu, sleep helps more than anything else. When I'm overwhelmed, it's often because I'm tired, not because I have too much to do (plus, getting some sleep first helps me then be more discerning about what I actually have to do and what I really don't need to do). When I'm stuck on a problem in our business or in my life, I sleep on it. When I can't seem to eat enough food (usually carbs) to make me feel satisfied, it's sleep I need, not potato chips.

Nearly everything is better after a solid nap and/or a good night's rest.

I say that sleep is my spiritual practice because when I'm well rested I can instantly remember who I am and what matters. I'm more resilient. I'm healthier. I'm more present. I'm happier. And I feel more connected to God/Goddess.

If you're looking to maximize your waking hours, you really need to sleep. Choosing to sleep an extra one to two hours and sacrificing those one to two hours of "productive time" will likely make you more productive during the time you do have the next day. And, over time, if you keep up the habit of getting enough sleep, you'll find that you get way more done in less time because you have higher brainpower, a better memory, and an increased ability to focus. Yay for doing less!

Sleep is the ultimate way to do less and have more. Here are a few tips to try that have to do with better sleep:

- Go to bed one hour earlier for a week and see how you feel.

- Try yoga nidra.

- Stop screen time two hours before bedtime. (Phones, TVs, tablets, and computers emit a blue light that makes it hard to get a good night's sleep for a variety of reasons.)[6]

- Go to bed and wake up at the same time every day for a week.

- Leave your phone plugged in overnight outside your bedroom.

- The next time you're tired, take a nap or go to bed.

You'll be amazed at how prioritizing this simple daily requirement allows you to have vastly more productivity in basically every area of your life.

experiment

10

become a time bender

We were in Los Angeles and had to get from one end of the city to another during rush hour. We had 30 minutes to get somewhere that it would have taken us an hour to get to if traffic were moving steadily.

I was super stressed out about getting there on time, but Mike told me to just get into the passenger's seat and he would take care of it.

We had to be there at 5:30 P.M., and we rolled up at 5:29. We'd been in flow the entire drive and somehow had managed to bend time and get there when we needed to get there.

Magic.

Time bending is a kind of everyday magic that you can use to not feel so stressed, not feel so rushed, and make the most of the time we have here on earth (at least this time around).

I was first introduced to the concept of time bending (though I don't think he calls it that) in Gay Hendricks's book *The Big Leap* (which is one of my top book picks of all time). Hendricks introduces the concept of Einstein time versus Newtonian time—essentially the same thing as chiros versus chronos, which we talked about earlier.

Einstein time: time that is relative and that you can stretch or shrink at your will depending on your perception, what you're doing, and your energy.

Newtonian time: linear time that we measure in set increments with clocks.

The idea in time bending is to get outside of linear, Newtonian time as much as possible and transport ourselves into relative Einstein time as often as possible.

What's awesome about being a mom is that you have these little people around you who tend to live in a timeless world anyway. So they are great teachers.

My daughter Penelope doesn't know when music class starts on Tuesday morning, and she doesn't care. She doesn't care that trying on five different dresses before she finds the one that is just right is going to make us late for music class. She's in the moment, feeling how the dresses lie against her skin, sensing into which one is right for today.

She loves music class when we're there, but she also loves doing what we're doing when we're doing it and she's not thinking about the other things we're going to do when she's doing the thing in front of her.

I've found the timelessness of hanging out with my small child to be one of the hardest, yet most rewarding, aspects of motherhood. When I can make the shift from Newtonian time, where I'm trying to rush us out the door to get somewhere or trying to get food in the oven at a certain time or trying to get some specific task done by a certain time, and instead move into Einstein time, where my girl and I are the source of time and we're just hanging, it's a freaking miracle. And it feels sooooo good. Like we're perched on this pink cloud of presence where all is well, there's nothing else in the world to worry about, and we have everything we need.

The only true way to slow down time is to fully inhabit the present moment. And our kids are born knowing how to do it. (So were we, by the way. We just got conditioned out of our timeless nature. But it's still in there. And I'm going to remind you how to tap into it.)

When you want to become a time bender, the first thing is to realize that there are, in fact, two different kinds of time and that you can experience time differently when you shift your perception and energy in the moment.

I know Einstein time and Newtonian time are just theoretical right now, but I want you to make them real for yourself, so do me a favor. Think about the last time you were totally in the moment doing something and you lost track of time because you were so absorbed in what you were doing.

Were you working on a project that got you firing on all cylinders and fed your soul and time stood still?

Was it chopping vegetables and getting into the zone?

Was it a great conversation with a girlfriend over tea where time seemed to suspend and it didn't even occur to you to wonder how much time had passed?

These are the moments that make a life. Not the 15 minutes we spend in the morning trying to rush our kids out the door so that everyone gets where they're going on time. Not the morning commute where you're trying to be anywhere but stuck in traffic. Not the after-dinner rush to do the dishes, get teeth brushed, get everyone in jammies, and finally have a moment of peace to yourself.

Nope. Those aren't the moments you're going to remember. It's the ones in between. It's the timeless ones. It's the ones where you are where you are and aren't trying to be somewhere else. Those are the ones that matter.

Time bending is partially about creating more of those moments so that your life fills you up instead of leaving you empty. It's also about becoming the source of time so that you feel like you have more than enough time to do the things that you want to do. And, yes, occasionally it's about speeding time up when you're doing something that you don't want to be doing and you wish it would be over soon.

Now that you've grasped that there's more to time than trying to race a clock, let's look at how to actually change your relationship to time.

Time Poverty vs. Time Prosperity

There's so much overlap between the way we relate to money and the way we relate to time. It's bananas.

If you took my first book, *Money: A Love Story*, and replaced the word *money* with *time* at each mention of it, you'd basically have your guidebook for how to create a more prosperous relationship with time and an experience of more than enough of it.

Just like with money, if we want to have the experience of more than enough time, we must start with how we think about time and what our relationship to it is.

Do you find yourself talking about time running out a lot? About not having enough time? About wishing there were more hours in the day?

Do you rush all the time? Do you feel like you're a slave to time?

These are all indications that you're living in time poverty. It's time to switch into time prosperity.

First off, simply notice what you think about time and what you say about time, especially around your kids. Kids are sponges, and when you're stressed about time, they'll pick up on it and either adopt your same stressed-out relationship with time or rebel against it, making you all late more often and stressing you out even more!

You'll be amazed by how you can make miraculous shifts in your experience of time simply by changing the way you think about it and the way you talk about it. When you stop affirming a lack of time, you'll stop experiencing a lack of time. It's pretty freaking remarkable.

Since this book is about doing small experiments, rather than deciding you're going to completely overhaul your relationship with time, give yourself a week. Simply decide that for a week you're going to suspend your disbelief and see what happens when you choose to live in time prosperity instead of time poverty.

See how your experience of time during this week is different from your experience of time during other weeks simply by making the decision to see what it's like to relate to time differently.

Once you gather your data, you can decide if you prefer living in the land of time poverty like everyone else or if you prefer the land of time prosperity. Totally up to you!

Become the Source of Time

A really great mantra that I like to use when I'm feeling rushed or like I don't have enough time is:

I am the source of time.

I've found that when I'm rushing around trying to do too many things at once or trying to fit too many things into my schedule, I end up knocking my coffee over and then having to take the extra time to clean it up and change my shirt and blot it out of the floor mat in my car. Plus, I forget things and have to come back home to get them. Then I'm all spazzed out and in this space of rushing so I do silly things like miss the exit on the highway and have to spend an extra 10 minutes getting all turned around.

So, counterintuitively, rushing tends to take me more time than if I go about what I need to calmly and as though I have enough time.

That's where the mantra comes in.

When I find myself getting into that spazzy place where my ego thinks that rushing around is going to save time, I remind myself that I am, in fact, the source of time, and that the more calmly I go about things, the more time I have.

Affirming that we are the source of time makes it so. Plus, it's just true anyway. When we believe we don't have enough time, we rush and see the whole world through the lens of lack. So we have created the experience of not enough time. When we believe that we have more than enough time to do the things we need to do, we project that reality on the world, and our experience of the world shifts so that what we experience is, in fact, more than enough time.

Whether you think you have enough time or not, either way, you're right.

Be Where You Are

Being present is something I'm always working to improve in my life, just like every other working mother who has a lot on her plate, feels a bit tethered to technology, and has a big appetite for life.

Though it seems as though trying to fit more into my day and do multiple things at the same time is the solution to maximizing my time, in the same way that rushing actually costs us more time than it gains us, trying to do too much (and too many things at the same time) usually robs us of time instead of giving us our time back. To truly have the experience of having more than enough time and fully enjoying the time we have, we have to be where we are and do less.

This morning, Penelope wanted to hold my hand as I was making coffee and making oatmeal. In the mornings, I find myself wanting to rush through the routine and get her fed and dressed and myself fed and dressed and everyone off to their respective places so we can get the day started.

But this morning, I remembered: This moment right here is my day. My day is already happening. I'm not waiting for it to start. It's started, and this little peanut wanting to hold my hand is part of it.

So I held hands with her and slowed down the whole process. Making coffee with one hand is harder, but it's way sweeter with my girl by my side.

Then she wanted to eat her oatmeal while sitting on my lap. And it turned out that she wanted me to feed it to her. And in the middle of it, she decided we should also read some books between bites.

None of this was in my morning plan. But when I sank into it and decided to fully inhabit the moment sitting with her on the floor with the oatmeal and the books, it was so sweet! I have no idea how long we were sitting on the floor reading pages in between bites and snuggling, but it didn't matter because I know it will be one of my favorite moments of this day.

Tonight, when I write in my *Mom's One Line a Day* memory journal, I won't recall the time I spent shooting off some e-mails while P played by herself in the other room (though that was time well spent too). I'll write down the sweet oatmeal/book picnic we had on the floor and how I entered my little girl's timeless world for a bit and it was delicious and magical.

I'm no expert on being present, but I've been to enough yoga classes, personal growth seminars, and meditation events to have gathered a few things that help me inhabit the present moment and, therefore, expand time.

Here they are:

Breathe: When I find myself rushing or wanting to hop out of the moment I'm in for whatever reason, I come back to noticing my breath. Sometimes I slow it down, but really all it takes is noticing it to come back to where I am.

Use the five senses: One of the easiest ways for me to come back to what's happening right in front of me is through my five senses. If I take a moment to notice what I'm seeing, smelling, touching, hearing, and tasting, I'm instantly right where I am and there's plenty going on to keep me engaged.

Come back to the body: The breath and the sense are really part of this, but overall if I remind myself to come back into my body I find myself in the present moment. I feel my butt on the chair. I notice the temperature of the room. I feel how good it feels to have my toddler's warm little body in my lap or to have Mike's hand in mine. And suddenly here I am: right here, where I am. And I don't want to be any other place.

The ingenious thing about being present is that it's a total shortcut to doing less. When we're really present, we aren't so obsessed with needing to do more. We find more satisfaction in small things, and we are more easily able to unhook from the false promise that more (doing or stuff or status) will actually bring us more joy. In fact, the complete opposite is true. Less doing and more being here where we are will bring us more joy. So if we start with being here where we are, we reduce the craving for more, and then we don't even have to try to do less. It just happens on its own, which is the best kind of doing less there is!

A Word on Technology

One thing that will suck your time and presence in one fell swoop is technology. I love and honor technology for how connected it allows us to be, how I can run a seven-figure business from home in my yoga pants, and how it allows us all to have a bigger platform and impact than we ever could have before it existed. That being said, it's a great servant but a really scary master.

Researchers have linked the high we get from the instant gratification of texting and social media to a neurotransmitter in our brain called dopamine, which is the same chemical related to heroin, cocaine, and alcohol abuse. It has to do with the pleasure and reward pathway in the brain, and while I'm no neuroscientist, I too feel the at times addictively compelling nature of my phone and the instant gratification of likes, comments, and texts that it delivers, not to mention the sheer delight of typing a search phrase like "dopamine and social media" into Google and getting instant results to learn more!

Given how our phones and other devices interact with our brain chemistry, it can feel almost unavoidable to pick up your phone and check it. On average, millennials check their phones 150 times a day.[1] I bet if you counted, your number wouldn't be that far off from that. (I'm raising my hand with you!)

And while technology can forge deeper connections and give us access to information we never would have had access to before, it can be at the cost of forging deeper connections with the people we're actually sitting next to.

I'll never forget one night after dinner, Mike and I were in the car (before having kids) and he said to me, "Sometimes I feel like I have to compete with your phone for your attention." Ugh. The reality of that statement was so awful to admit. I knew he was right, and I decided to make a concerted effort to be more present.

Technology is incredibly distracting and can suck your productivity right out of the day. Researchers estimate that it takes us nearly 25 minutes to get refocused on a task when we've gotten distracted[2] and that we spend an average of 11 minutes on a project before getting distracted.[3]

So if you do the math, that means you're spending zero minutes totally focused on what you're doing. And if you're constantly either getting distracted or trying to get refocused (which massively increases levels of stress and overwhelm and feelings of pressure), you're never present and you're certainly not able to feel like you're the source of time.

Obviously, there are distractions, like your kids and co-workers interrupting you, which you have less control over, but you are actually in charge of your technology, not the other way around. I'm definitely a work in progress when it comes to detaching from technology and tuning in more deeply to what or who is in front of me in the actual world, but I have noticed a few things that have really made a difference in terms of digital boundaries in my life.

Here they are, should you care to adopt any for yourself and your family:

We plug our phones into a charging station in a drawer in the kitchen around 8 P.M. and turn them on airplane mode. We don't bring our phones into the bedroom unless we have an early flight and need an alarm. (We don't have an alarm clock in our room at this point because we have a toddler who rarely sleeps past 6 A.M. and does a great job of waking us up in the morning.) That's the only time a phone enters our bedroom.

I keep my phone on silent almost all day every day. I cannot stand notification noises or buzzing or the phone ringing because it throws me off course from what I'm doing. When I'm focused on something, I turn my phone over so I can't see the screen (because the light in the corner of my eye and little things that pop up are distracting even if they don't make noise). I basically never pick up the phone (and really never if it's a number I don't recognize), and my outgoing message even says that I never listen to voice mail, so if they'd like to hear back from me they should send a text.

I have almost no notifications turned on on my phone. So when my screen is locked, it's just locked, and I don't have a million little gremlins trying to get my attention every time I look at it. I decide when I'm going to look at certain apps. I'm in control of my time (I am the source of time), not the app developers.

I keep my computer on silent most of the day. I don't have little notifications popping up or little noises alerting me of things. I am doing what I'm doing, and when I decide it's time to do something else, then I'll decide that, not a little beep or flashing icon.

I turn off almost all notifications on my computer so that when I'm working on something, I'm not getting pulled to look at something else.

I keep my phone in my purse or away from the table at mealtime. No phones out. Period.

(Mike and I saw a group of teenagers out for dinner a while back and they all had their cell phones turned face-down in the middle of the table in a pile. We asked them what was up with that, and they told us that whoever went to grab their phone first during the meal had to pay for everyone else's dinner. Those kids gave me hope for the future of humanity.)

I do my best to keep my phone in my purse when I'm in the passenger seat and Mike is driving. This is one of the most challenging times for me because it feels like "in-between time" that doesn't really count. But I spent 10 months driving around the country with Mike, and I know how much meaningful connection can happen while we're both looking out the windshield in the same direction sitting side by side. And when I'm on my phone, I miss the moment for that. So I keep working on this one.

I'm always working on keeping my phone turned over and away when I'm with my daughters. This one is totally a work in progress, but it's on my radar and I catch myself more and more, so I think that counts for a lot. Progress, not perfection!

When you decide to become a time bender, you decide to be in control of your time rather than your time controlling you. And this, my dear, is an incredibly powerful place to be. Your life is made up of nothing more than years, days, hours, minutes, and seconds. And she who is in control of how she invests these precious increments of time is truly blessed with a life that feels like her own and that feels well lived. What else is there, anyway?

experiment

11

streamline your to-do list

You know the satisfaction you get from checking something off of your to-do list? You know what makes it even more satisfying? When you don't have a million things on the list that don't get done because your eyes were bigger than your schedule!

Traditional time management and productivity systems are really built around the premise that if you can manipulate your schedule and your activities enough, you'll be able to cram more into a day. And while that's all fine and good, I've yet to read a study that cramming more into your day makes you feel happier or more fulfilled.

None of the regrets of the dying include not having crammed more into their days.

I like to approach my to-do list from a totally different perspective based on how I feel and how I want to feel. I've been charting my course in life based on knowing that I want to choose to do the thing that makes me feel the best because feeling good is the whole point anyway. And over the years I've refined this process to include my do less philosophy so that everything works together.

I used to write a to-do list every single day, but I would end up putting about 10 different tasks (or more) on it and never getting more than a few things done a day. So every day would end and I would feel like I'd fallen short. Then the next morning I would write a new to-do list and transfer everything I hadn't done from the day before to the new day's list as well as add new things as they came up.

I was left with this never-ending to-do list that, when I looked at it, made me feel overwhelmed and defeated.

I also had a friend who taught me her system of capturing all of her to-dos, which involved a book and five different highlighters and color coding and keeping a running log of literally everything you could think of to ever do and not quitting until it was all done. While I enjoyed the color coding, using this system made me feel like a slave to the book and like I was constantly behind.

Then I tried David Allen's *Getting Things Done* method of spending a few days gathering all projects and to-dos from your entire life and then getting them into his intricate system of lists for separate things. I never got it all set up, for one thing, and the idea of keeping the whole thing going and figuring out which list an item was supposed to go on and then checking all of those lists made me feel like I was drowning in to-dos, not to mention the complexity of the system itself. (No offense to *GTD* devotees or David Allen. You do you.)

I really, really, really like Abraham-Hicks's ongoing reminder in their books and audios that we're never going to get it all done. Every time/productivity management system I've ever tried (before the one I'm about to share with you) seemed based on the illusion that someday I'd actually get everything done if I followed the system perfectly. But no matter how we're managing our to-dos and no matter how well we schedule our time, we will never get it all done.

While this may sound defeating to some, it feels wildly freeing to me. If my overarching philosophy is that I'm never going to get it all done anyway, I can loosen my grip on my to-do list and just have fun. We can all relax a little, guys. No one is checking to see how much we got done when we die. There's no parade. There's not going to be an awards ceremony or a big check to cash for the person who did the most.

So if we know we're never going to get it all done anyway, how can we approach our to-do lists with sanity and spaciousness?

I'm so glad you asked, because I'm about to tell you.

Weekly vs. Daily

Over a year ago, I started writing a weekly to-do list instead of a daily one. There were so many more unexpected elements in my day, so many more things that were out of my control as a mother than ever before. And while I used to wake up and have pretty much exclusive control over my day, I no longer felt that way after having kids.

So the way I approached my time had to shift. Instead of digging my claws into what I would get done in a day, I decided to get really realistic and graceful about what I would get done in a week. I've heard a lot of people say that when they became a parent they had to lower their expectations of themselves in terms of what they could get done. But I choose to see it as simply having changed my expectations of myself.

In fact, I've found that because I'm way more focused and I have no time to screw around, I actually get a lot more done than I did before having kids. Or at least I get more results from what I'm actually doing. I'm not sure exactly which it is, but either way it feels like a win.

I've also shifted my expectations of myself in terms of how long I'm going to have to get any one task done, how many "extras" I have space for in my life, like side projects and hobbies, and how my day is going to go. Often, I have no idea what's going to happen in a day, and releasing my need to control it has been the most sanity-giving thing of all.

To account for the fact that every day of motherhood is different and I don't have the same control over my time that I used to (though I do have total control over my perception of my time, and I rock that control like a red carpet gown), I make my to-do list weekly instead of daily. I like that it feels more spacious, more holistic, and more "gestalt." Instead of obsessing about what happens in 24 hours, I have an intention about what will happen over the course of seven days. And when I get really clear on what actually needs to happen within a period of seven days (using the strategies I'm about to share with you), it usually actually happens. It's a freaking miracle.

I can honestly say that about 80 percent of the time these days I actually cross off every item on my weekly to-do list. What this tells me is not that I'm somehow cramming a ton into my day and winning at productivity. What this tells me is that I've finally gotten good at knowing what I can do in a week and, most important, knowing what to leave off the list.

If you want to feel instantly saner, make a weekly to-do list instead of a daily one. You're welcome.

Body, Mind, Heart, Cosmos

Most time management systems come exclusively from the head. They're all based on what needs to happen to move the needle forward and grow and get better and advance and win! It comes from the intellect and the intellect alone.

The way I like to approach my to-do list is from my body, mind, and heart and then also include the cosmos as I'm consciously curating what makes it onto my to-do list. I see my to-do list as a sacred space, so not everything deserves a place there. My time is precious. My energy is precious. Only the most worthy of tasks make it on the list. I use my to-do list as a way that I honor and love myself, and I invite you to do the same.

I write my to-do list for the week on Sunday evenings, and I love the practice of looking at my week and making any adjustments I need to make ahead of time. It feels really loving to be proactive about my time rather than reactive. When I sit down to make my list, I use my Origin Planner, which includes a page I call the Weekly Renewable Planner. This has a mandala that includes four areas to guide your week and your to-do list:

- Body: How's your energy this week? What phase of your cycle are you in?

- Mind: What are your top three priorities for the week?

- Heart: How do you feel? How do you want to feel?

- Cosmos: What's going on with the moon, stars, and planets that might impact you this week?

Before I get into the due dates and tasks and projects that I have on my plate, I ground myself in my body, mind, heart, and the cosmos, because I know that how I feel matters the most. Not what I accomplish. And if I truly believe this (which I do), I have to plan my time from this place, not from the place of rushing to get more done and achieve more. So it is my weekly ritual that I plan my time around the things that matter most, and I trust that when I do this, the things that most need to happen will happen, and if something doesn't happen, it didn't matter that much anyway.

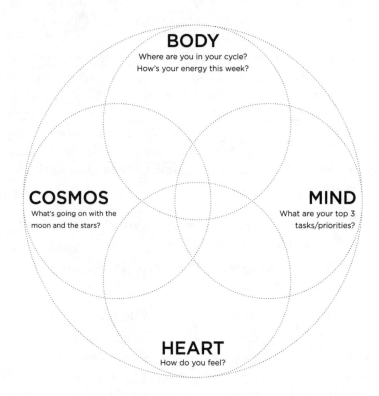

I always start with the body. When I start with my body in any area of my life, I am never steered wrong. I start my week by asking my body how she feels and what she most needs. If I'm cycling, I'll put which phase of my cycle I'm in. This is great information for me to keep in mind when I start tallying up items on my to-do list. I know if I'm in my follicular phase, I'll probably have a lot of energy for planning, brainstorming, and starting. If I'm in my ovulation phase, I know it's a great week for getting out there, reaching out to make connections, and communicating. If I'm in my luteal phase, I know my energy will be likely turning inward and this is a great week to focus on detailed work and really capitalizing on workhorse energy to finish up projects. And if I'm in my menstrual phase, I know that I'll want to go really easy on my to-dos and give myself space for rest, evaluation, and research this week.

(Remember: This is not a perfect science. Peppering even 10 to 20 percent of the ideal activities for the phase of our cycle into our to-do list is magnificent and will reap way more rewards than getting overwhelmed by it and thus not paying attention at all.)

If I'm not cycling, I'll put how many weeks pregnant I am (if I'm pregnant) or simply how my body is feeling that week so that I can honor that as I craft my to-do list. I also pay extra attention to the lunar phase in the cosmos section coming up, since that has the same four energetic phases as the menstrual cycle.

Next up is the mind. I ask myself what are my top three priorities based on which project I'm working on, which phase it's in (Emergence, Visibility, Culmination, or the Fertile Void), and what's coming up on the calendar. Creating content is always in there somewhere because that's at the top of my vital few, and then sometimes the other two things are business-related or sometimes they're more personal.

For example, last week my top three priorities were to work on this book, finish the poinsettia fund-raiser for Penelope's school, and batch content for our upcoming two-week company holiday break.

When I write out my top three priorities and keep those at the top of my radar, I give myself permission to be more relaxed about all of the other to-dos that are also on my radar but don't get as much bandwidth. Also, when I know my top three and it's a week where I have a sick kid or I'm super exhausted or we lose power for five days (like we did a few weeks ago), I know the bare minimum that needs to get done in the limited time that I end up having to do it.

I've already decided that if I attend to my top three priorities in any given week, then that week was a success. It doesn't matter if there are 15 other things that didn't get my attention. I know what's the most important, and I feel like a rock star as long as it got done to the best of my ability that week.

Three things for the week. That's it. Give it a try and see how awesome you feel.

Next is the heart and how you feel at the beginning of the week and how you want to feel. I include how I want to feel and how I'm actually feeling in the moment when I'm making my to-do list. If I'm overwhelmed or anxious, I'll make a note of that and see how I can shift that feeling as I make my list and start off my week.

For example, we're about to go on vacation this coming week, so I know I want to feel relaxed and really present with Mike, Penelope, and Ruby. I use these as my guidepost for the week and return to them time and time again.

Finally, we turn to the cosmos and ask what's in store for us from that angle this week. I'm not a believer in using astrological events as an excuse. ("Well, Mercury is in retrograde and everything is going to be totally screwed up communication- and technology-wise anyway, so why even bother doing anything?") Instead, I like to use it as an additional piece of information so that I can best capitalize on the energetic forces around me to support my life.

There are a lot of astrologers who will give a weekly cosmic weather report and I recommend reading a few to see which one's style you like the best as there are so many different flavors out there. Our resident astrologer in Origin is Jennifer Racioppi, and I really love her take on things because she looks through the lens of feminine leadership. She gives us a cosmic weather report every month so that we can use it as we lay out how we'll devote our time and energy that month. We can take advantage of auspicious aspects for our work lives, motherhood, relationships, and more. I love knowing that the Universe has my back in this way if I'm willing to pay attention and work with her.

A key aspect of what's going on in the cosmos is what phase the moon is in. I love paying attention to the moon because I know I'm going to be affected by it whether I'm aware of it or not. I figure knowledge is power, so I might as well work with her rather than her just working me.

When I know what phase the moon is in or what other astrological aspects are going on, I give myself more grace when things feel wonky. I don't beat myself up as much (or at all), which is awesome because beating ourselves up is a colossal waste of energy! Also, when you're not cycling, tracking the lunar phases is a powerful way to remember your cyclical nature and tap into a creative cycle that's impacting your body all the time anyway. When you embrace it, you'll be amazed by how held you feel, how much more synchronistic your life becomes, and how much more magical things feel.

Now that you've spent some time paying attention to your body, mind, heart, and the cosmos, it's time to write your to-do list for the week.

Your To-Do List

So what goes on your to-do list? First off, if you make your to-do list your brain dump of anything and everything that ever might need to get done by you or anyone else in your immediate vicinity, you will be out before you've even started. This is a recipe for overwhelm and, honestly, working motherhood disaster.

The key here is conscious curation. In fact, what you leave off your to-do list is almost more important than what you put on there.

That's why I recommend asking your body, mind, heart, and the cosmos what's up before you just dive in and start writing things down.

When I used to use my to-do list as a brain dump, I was trying to use it as an anxiolytic. But your to-do list is not the place to go with an anxious mind to try to calm down by letting the list become the catchall for your worries. If you do it this way, every time you come back to the list you'll be met with the very same kind of anxiety that made the list. And then you'll be back at square one again.

Instead, you want to be super persnickety about what makes it on the list. This is your sacred space. It's your life. Your life is made up of what you do on a weekly basis. So make it mindful.

When I write my to-do list for the week, I look at what's coming up in the calendar like due dates, I look at where I am in various projects, and then I make the list. If this list is longer than one-half of an 8.5 x 11–inch page then it's too long. It's extremely rare that I'll get everything done on a list that does fill that space, anyway, so if it's longer, ain't no way it's all happening.

Before I write each item down, I like to do a quick inventory of the following questions:

- Does this need to be done?

- Does this need to be done by me?

- Does this need to be done right now?

The first one is kind of obvious. If it doesn't need to be done, just don't write it down. This question offers you a great opportunity to check your assumptions about what is and isn't necessary. When you're asking it, think about the desired result of this particular action step or the group of action steps that it goes with to make up a project. Is this action step truly necessary to get that result, or even a result that's really close to the desired result? Be ruthless here. If the answer is no, can it.

The second one is a great opportunity to go back to what we talked about in Experiment #6 about your mind-set around and ability to ask for help. If the item could be done by someone else to even 80 percent the effectiveness that you could do it, delegate it. A woman who knows how to delegate is a woman who knows how to create freedom.

The third one is tricky and gets into a bigger conversation about the order of things. If you have two deadlines coming up, but one comes before the other, it probably makes more sense to write the tasks you need to do for the deadline that's sooner on your to-do list for any given week and finish that project up before you get started on the next one.

I can find myself slipping back into the old brain dump in order to ease anxiety habits sometimes when I'm making my to-do list for the week and just putting down tasks I think of that really don't need to be done for another few weeks. Putting them on my list makes me feel this false sense of puffed-up hope and pride that I'll get more done in a week than I actually know I can do. And then I just have to keep transferring the tasks until they really need to be done. It's silly and, honestly, a waste of time.

(You can keep a separate master list of projects and tasks if you're afraid you'll forget things that need to get done in future weeks. We do this with our team in our project management software, Teamwork, but you can simply use Evernote, the Notes section on your phone, or a project management software or list building app like Asana or Wunderlist.)

Instead, asking myself, *Does this really need to be done right now?* or *Does this really need to be done this week?* is a great way to keep myself honest and focused on what's in front of me rather than getting too caught up in what's coming weeks from now. Staying focused on just what needs to happen this week not only gives me more energy to get done the things that need to happen because I'm not overwhelmed every time I look at my list, it also gives me a great sense of satisfaction when I get my reasonable list of things done by the end of the week (most of the time). And that sense of satisfaction gives me more energy that I can use as fuel for the following week!

The Opposite Is Also True

Now, only doing the things that need to be done right now could get you trapped in the urgent/not-important cesspool that Stephen Covey talks about in *The 7 Habits of Highly Effective People* when he introduces the concept of the Decision Matrix (also known as the Eisenhower Matrix).

THE EISENHOWER MATRIX

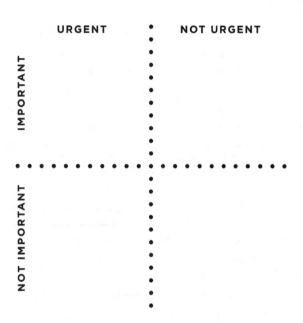

Urgent/important tasks would be things like going to your crying baby, a fire in your kitchen, or your best friend calling to tell you that her mother just passed away. You have to deal with them, they matter, and you have to deal with them right now.

Urgent/not-important tasks are things like most phone calls, most e-mails, most interruptions, and almost all social media notifications. You *think* you have to deal with them right now, but in most cases, you don't, and in most cases, they don't matter that much to the grand vision of your life.

Non-urgent/important tasks are things like your health, your relationships, and your dreams. We often ignore these things until it's too late, but they're the most important parts of our lives, and without giving the things in this quadrant regular nurturing, our lives feel meaningless and we forget to fulfill our dreams.

Non-urgent/not-important tasks are things like busywork or other things that waste our time, but the good news is that most people don't spend very much time in this quadrant, so I wouldn't worry about it too much (unless you get way bogged down in things like intricate filing systems or creating complications where there need be none).

What's interesting to note is that we tend to spend the majority of our time on the urgent/not-important tasks because they present themselves as fires and we fancy ourselves firefighters. They trigger our fight-or-flight response, and we jump into action to solve the problem before taking a moment to even ask ourselves if this problem is ours to solve, if it's even worth solving, or if it's even a problem to begin with.

Social media notifications are a great example of this. They're urgent because they're flashing in red and they beep at us, but in the grand scheme of moving our lives forward and delivering profound meaning, they're not important. (A great app for getting a reality check on how much time you actually spend on social media and other apps like games, and putting a cap on it, is called In Moment.)

E-mails are another great example. You get a tone on your computer and the little icon flashes, and before you even know what you're doing, you're helping your friend from high school gather a bunch of information that she asked you for, which she could have easily found herself on Google. Urgent but not important, at least not to you.

That's why knowing what matters to you, like we identified in Experiment #2, and knowing your vital few, like we identified in Experiment #4, is so critical. Without this information to guide your ship, you're rudderless and will jump at any opportunity to be in action completely indiscriminately because we're all programmed that busy is better, no matter what it is we're actually doing. But we know better, ladies. And so we must do better. (Or do less, as the case may be.)

So as you create your weekly to-do list, make sure that at least one or two items on there are from the non-urgent/ important category, and, of course, as you get better and better at doing less, you can add more things from that category to the list so that most of your time is spent on the things that mean the most to you and that make the most difference in your life and the lives of others.

The Universe's To-Do List

Finally, but possibly most important, don't forget to get the Universe on your side when it comes to your weekly to-do list. This weekly practice is inspired by the book *Ask and It Is Given* by Abraham-Hicks, which is an amazing book on surrendering and attracting things rather than working your tush off for them.

You do not have to do everything yourself (hopefully you're starting to understand that). And you know what— sometimes you can delegate things to the Universe!

I included an entire half page the same size as my to-do list in my Origin Planner for the Universe's Weekly To-Do List because asking for cosmic support is just as important as getting clear on what we personally can do on the human plane. If we limit what can get done to our small, human existence, though, we're seriously restricting what's possible for us and the world.

On Sunday nights, when I sit down to craft my to-do list for the week, I always write at least one thing down for the

Universe. A recent example is that I was feeling overwhelmed and a little anxious about finding a new child-care situation for our daughter for Thursdays. Our previous arrangement wasn't working out, and though I'd asked around and posted in different Facebook groups, I was coming up short, so one week I decided to turn it over to the Universe and write it down on the other side of my sheet of paper.

A few days after I delegated Thursday child care to the Universe, the director of our day care told me she'd heard we'd been looking for care for Penelope and that she had Thursdays off and would love to spend the day with P. What a godsend! Penelope adored this woman, I trusted her, and she loved Penelope. Done and done!

Any time I'm feeling stressed out about a particular project or task or I'm feeling doubt start to creep in about my capacity to will something to happen, I make sure I write it on the Universe's To-Do List. Now, that doesn't mean I won't also take a few action steps toward it, but it does mean I've let go of my need to be the only one responsible for it and I've allowed space for miracles and manifestation.

For example, during a big promotion in our business, I'll put the final financial or enrollment goal on the Universe's To-Do List column so that I don't feel like I have to hold it by myself. Then I'll go about my tasks for the launch, like writing promotional e-mails, doing Facebook lives, etc. Turning it over helps remind me that there's infinite help available to me, that the world is truly magical and abundant, and that I get to access that as long as I'm willing to ask. I personally love this practice, and I invite you to incorporate it into your week, especially when you're feeling overwhelmed and limited by the number of hours that you have in a day.

You don't have to do it all, my dear. Not by a long shot. There's help. There's so much help. Let go and let the magic unfold.

open the lines
of communication

I lay there in the pitch blackness of our bedroom, black-out shades drawn against the unreasonably bright streetlight in our front yard, which drenched the porch in daylight-level brightness between sunrise and sunset.

He said he was going to work out. Would I mind waking up with Penelope? I had said yes, that was fine. But the truth is it wasn't fine. I had been looking forward to sleeping in on this particular Friday all week. Just over a year of being up several times a night (except for the odd few weeks here and there where she'd miraculously sleep through the night) and also often being woken up way before my body was ready had left me tired on a level I previously hadn't known existed. Even my bone marrow desperately needed a nap.

We had been halfheartedly doing our regular scheduling conversations, and so things were slipping through the cracks. Assumptions were being made. Resentments were building. Things were going unsaid, and the water had seeped into the crack, now freezing as the weather turned colder and expanding the fissure into an ugly, unwieldy frost heave right down the middle of our marriage.

I was pissed. He was pissed. Both of us felt unheard and unappreciated. Both of us were exhausted. Both of us had needs that weren't getting met. We recognized the need to do something about it early, luckily. When a fight about stuffed peppers turned into three days of frost between us, we saw that perhaps we needed help, and beyond going to see a somatic therapist (which got us out of the content and into what our tension was truly about—hallelujah for the body trip that is somatic therapy and all body-based practices), we instituted a series of checks and balances to keep our marriage and family on the same page.

You know what I wish women did less of? Resenting their partners for not participating enough, not showing up enough, and not helping out more. And you know what really helps? Communicating what it is we need in order to feel supported. No one can give us what we want unless we tell them what it is. While there's this idea out there that true love means someone can magically read your mind and meet all of your needs without you having to speak up, it's completely bogus, and if you're waiting for that, prepare to be waiting forever.

Lack of communication is the cause of so much unnecessary drama and angst in our lives. If you want to do less rushing, do less stressing, and do less resenting of your spouse or other key people in your life, I recommend getting proactive. There are a few simple practices that Mike and I do like clockwork that, in addition to a good therapist every now and again, I'm quite sure are the secret to our relationship working.

It's Not About the Stuffed Peppers

Before we dive into the logistical practices that have been lifesavers for us, I want to talk about marriage for a hot minute.

As I write this, I've been with my husband for almost seven years, and we've been married for three and a half of those years. We've essentially lived together since our first kiss and we've been running a business together unofficially since 2011 but officially since 2013.

I come from a divorced family (my parents were married 24 years before going their separate ways), and romantic love has always been a top priority for me. Studying what does and doesn't work in relationships has always been a passion, probably because I really wanted to create something that I didn't get to witness growing up.

In order for any of the logistical stuff I'm about to introduce to work in your relationship and family, we have to all agree on one thing first:

It's not about the stuffed peppers.

A while back, Mike and I were talking about what was for dinner, and somehow we ended up in a really intense argument that started out having something to do with stuffed peppers. As is often the case, I really have no idea what we thought we were fighting about or what the issue actually was, but I remember how awful it felt and how I didn't want to talk to Mike, let alone see him afterward, because I was so deeply triggered by it.

I called my dear friend Terri Cole, a psychotherapist and top-level bullshit detector, and she helped walk me out of my heart-pounding anger and into a place of understanding that the incident had nothing to do with stuffed peppers but was instead connected to my deep wound around not feeling supported and Mike's deep wound around feeling like he was not enough. The stuffed pepper incident came after a long string of arguments (none of them this explosive, but still noteworthy) where we both were left feeling disconnected, triggered, and like the other person was out to get us. This wasn't what I'd had in mind for my marriage, and I knew we needed to do something about it before whatever had infected our bond metastasized.

Sadly, Terri is too dear of a friend to be our therapist, so I got a referral from another friend to a guy she said had made a huge positive impact in her marriage. I'd laid my cards on the table early on in my relationship with Mike when it seemed like he might be my guy and told him that one of my ground rules was that if we ever needed it, he had to be willing to go see a therapist with me.

So here I was pulling the therapy card only two years into our marriage. We'd hit a stalemate and kept ending up in the same argument, circling the same triggers, pushing the same buttons. We'd sit on opposite ends of the living room on couches, which with only five feet between them, felt like they were miles apart. And both of our hearts were hurting.

While he was resistant at first, Mike came right around because he realized if he was having trouble with his car, he would see a mechanic. If he was having trouble with his dead-lift, he would see a lifting coach. If he wanted to learn how to better optimize webinars, he would hire an expert. We were having trouble in our marriage and we didn't know how to fix it. So we got outside help. (If you have a partner, especially one who was raised with toxic ideas of masculinity—e.g., men are weak if they ask for help—perhaps this perspective shift will help.)

Within 20 minutes of the first session, we saw our pattern so clearly. We saw an even deeper level of what Terri had helped me understand, which was that Mike was triggering an original wound I had about not feeling supported and I was triggering in Mike an original wound about not feeling like he was enough. And the more I felt unsupported by him and said so, the less he felt like he was enough. And the less enough he felt, the more unsupported I felt. It was an icky cycle.

Rather than stay in the loop of blaming the other person for the challenges we were having in our marriage, we were able to actually connect with the parts of ourselves that were stuck in childhood hurts, which were getting triggered and running our central nervous systems as adults. We were able to soothe them, explain that we were handling things now as our adult selves, that they were safe, and that they could just go back to doing their kid things.

I know that this might sound silly and overly simplified, but I swear to you within 20 minutes of our first session I was able to soften and see Mike through the eyes of love again after weeks of feeling like we were in a disconnected stalemate. Plus, I will never forget the moment sitting across the living room from him after one of our arguments where we found ourselves back in the loop of me not feeling supported and him not feeling like he was enough, when I realized that there was literally nothing Mike could do in order to make me feel supported enough to heal the childhood wound in me that didn't feel supported. And, conversely, there was nothing I could do, no matter how many times I told him I believed in him and he was enough, that could heal his childhood wound of not feeling like he was enough.

We had both been waiting in desperation for the other person to fill the support and enough sized holes, respectively, and I realized if we kept waiting for the other one to fix it for us, it would never be fixed. We would be helplessly waiting for each other to make ourselves whole forever. In the moment I realized that I was the only one who could convince my little girl that she was supported and safe, the ice between Mike and me melted, the frost heave smoothed out, and I actually wanted to be near him again. I got off my couch, crossed the five feet to his couch, snuggled up next to him, and promised to start feeling supported from the inside.

He promised to start feeling enough from the inside.

So there we were, finally meeting our own needs, together.

The Logistics of Love

Once you understand that you will likely choose life partners, business partners, and even close friends who will trigger your deepest wounds so that you have the opportunity to heal in a really profound way, and you step up and are willing to do that healing work (which, by the way, will continue for your entire life, so no need to get impatient about it), then you can move on to the logistics of living in partnership and family with others. (Your relationship with your own mother and even your mother-in-law can be amazingly fertile ground for personal healing as well. You know what they say: "If it's not one thing, it's your mother!")

If you don't first acknowledge that whatever conflicts arise between you and your partner are likely not about the content of the actual conflict, you're going to get caught in the trap of trigger loops, and you'll never be able to rise above blame and hurt. Logistical communication strategies are pathetic little Mickey Mouse Band-Aids adhered to gaping wounds when the trigger patterns in a relationship aren't also being addressed, but if the trigger patterns are being addressed (ideally with a great therapist, one who helps you tap into deeper layers of healing, like a somatic therapist, or at least great books like *Attached* and *Getting the Love You Need*), then logistical practices can be an ease-filled savior for your partnership and family as a whole.

Mike and I swear by four weekly practices that force us to overcommunicate and make sure that assumptions aren't made, that we both get the support we need, that logistics are handled with ease and don't become a cesspool of stress, and that we talk about what needs to be talked about.

Shared Calendar

As I mentioned, Mike and I share our calendars on Google Calendars. I see everything on his calendar and he sees everything on my calendar. If I have something that I'm doing that's related to a surprise or something that I don't want him to see for some other reason, like a gift, I simply name it something else or put "secret event."

Anytime I wonder where Mike is or what he has going on, I simply open my phone and there are all of his events in yellow on my calendar (my events are in purple). This helps immensely because I don't have to ask him what's going on. I simply check.

Sharing our calendars isn't enough, though. We also have a rule that if the other person needs to be present at one of the events we have scheduled, we need to send them a Google calendar invite, and we cannot assume that they'll see the event themselves and know they need to be present. (Obviously, we figured this one out the hard way.) If I've planned a date night, I send him a calendar invite. If he's scheduled a podcast interview with someone, he sends me a calendar invite. If we're meeting a carpenter to talk about putting shelves in our mudroom and Mike wants me to weigh in, he sends me a calendar invite.

I think we've saved ourselves hundreds of arguments with calendar invites. It's seriously the best thing ever because we don't have to rely on our ability to remember to tell the other person things when we're together in person. Game. Changer. Some families prefer to have a calendar up on the wall in the kitchen, where everyone can see it and add their own things. We may institute this as the kids get older, but for now I love having my calendar on my phone and on my computer so that no matter where I am, I know what's going on.

Weekly Meeting

One would think that the shared calendars and calendar invites would be enough to keep us on the same page as far as scheduling. And yet we still noticed that things were coming up unexpectedly, leaving one or the other of us feeling left in the lurch, disappointed, or unsupported. That's why we instituted our Monday-morning scheduling conversation where we talk through the week, day by day, to highlight what's coming up. We often realize during this conversation that we need to hire a babysitter that we've forgotten to hire, that I need to ask my mom to come watch Penelope for an hour to give us a grace period to get back from conflicting appointments, or that one or the other of us has made an appointment and forgotten to send a calendar invite. We'll usually look at the coming week with a fine-toothed comb and then give the next week an overview too, just so we have a good idea of what's going on in a chunk of two weeks.

I find that overcommunicating about scheduling, while it may seem overkill, is one of the keys to making our lives run smoothly. Neither of us feels like we're the only one "holding the bag" of the family schedule, and rather than having scheduling surprises come up that leave one or both of us scrambling, we can use the element of surprise in our relationship for unexpected gifts or a surprise date night that one of us plans that the other doesn't know about. (As our girls get older and have things going on that we might not know about, we'll definitely include them in the weekly scheduling portion of this meeting and perhaps to some degree in the #MoneyLove Date because I want them to grow up feeling empowered around their time and money, not dependent on us all the time.)

We also simply check in with one another. We see if anything has come up during the last week that needs to be talked about logistically or emotionally. Usually this part of the conversation is just a few minutes, but occasionally it's turned into an hour or more heart-to-heart that has not only prevented an argument down the line, but also left us both feeling more connected and more in love.

One woman in our Origin Collective is a therapist and is married to a therapist, and they have two kids. They also do a weekly meeting and have found that it's really helpful if they remind themselves at the beginning of sitting down together that both will get their needs met and that there's enough time and resources. So often, especially when we have young kids, both parents feel scarcity around their needs getting met, so agreeing to start with this mind-set at the outset of your meeting can be incredibly helpful for setting the tone and in fact creating an environment where both can get their needs met. This kind of weekly meeting is also super beneficial with employees, assistants, and colleagues at work to make sure everyone is on the same page and important tasks and communications don't get overlooked due to assumptions or lack of clarity.

#MoneyLove Date

We also have a weekly #MoneyLove Date that we used to have during our Monday-morning meeting but have recently moved because it was getting too rushed and Mike wasn't feeling as supported as he wanted around managing our finances (he's the lead person on that, but I participate quite a bit too because I don't believe in living in the dark about what's going on with your money, regardless of how well your partner manages it). I talk much more about this in my book *Money: A Love Story*, but the long and short of it is that by default, Mike and I are both money avoiders who love to spend and then not pay much attention to what's coming in or what's going out.

We've both done a ton of work on ourselves around our money and money mind-sets and have found that showing up together for our money once a week has been crucial for us to not only pay off hundreds of thousands in debt, but also to create the abundance that we feel so blessed to have created.

During our #MoneyLove Date, we look at what's in our business bank account, we transfer a set amount of money into another account for our personal needs, one for our personal wants, one for taxes, and one for savings. (Yes, we could make these transfers automatic, but since we're both money avoiders by nature, we like to do it manually because what we pay attention to grows and we don't want to space out!) Then we look at what other large expenses might be coming up, we talk about financial goals and see if we're on track and what might need adjusting, and we generally check in with what's going on with our money and how we're both feeling about it.

Once a month on the first of the month, we pay our credit cards and look over our reports from our bookkeeper that include an itemized list of all business expenses, our balance sheet, and our profit and loss statement (P&L). We also look at our personal expenses, which Mike tracks using mint .com. (We called all of our credit card companies and had the due dates moved to the first of the month so that it's all organized and we can batch this activity.)

Date Nights

The other night I was sitting at dinner with a group of my girlfriends from high school and their husbands. (I'm super blessed to be part of a group of nine women who have remained really close since childhood.) My dear friend was sitting on my right and was talking about starting a family. She's the last of us to have kids, and she was looking for any advice we have as she stands on the precipice of a whole different kind of life. (As we know, life is never the same after kids.)

My other girlfriend practically jumped across the table at her and said, "Take care of your marriage! Regular date nights are so key. Every day my son comes home from third grade and tells me about another kid in his class whose parents are splitting up. Your relationship needs to come first."

I'd also heard the same advice before having kids. In fact, when a friend with two kids told me that my relationship had to be a priority above my kids, I was a little shocked, and there was a part of me that questioned how good of a mother this friend was. Until I had my own kids. And then I got it.

Some couples swear by weekly date nights. Some make it monthly. Some alternate who plans it. Some have a standing date at the same place. Whatever works for you is great, but bottom line: Spend time with your partner without your kids. Your partnership will be better off. You won't wake up 20 years from now when your kids are out of the house and look across the table and wonder who the hell you shacked up with. And for sure your kids will be better off. Happy couples make happy families.

If you feel guilty about spending time with your partner away from your kids or work, I would recommend taking a deep look at what's driving that guilt. The belief that your kids will not be okay unless you're with them all the time will eventually take you down, and it's not good for them either.

If your partnership didn't work out for whatever reason, there's zero part of me that's blaming you or lack of date nights for that. My parents were married for 24 years, and then it was time for them to not be married anymore. It wasn't either of their fault, and neither of them considers their marriage a failure. It was a successful 24-year marriage. I don't think a weekly or monthly date night would have prevented their divorce, for the record. That being said, small investments in your relationship over time will amount to a boatload of difference in your intimacy, communication, and connectedness when your partnership is the right one for you both to be in at the right time.

Friends Always

When I first fell in love with my husband, I made a pact with myself to prioritize relationships with my friends always. No matter what. Why? Because expecting your romantic relationship to meet all of your emotional needs is not only unfair, it's guaranteed to disappoint you. We need more than our partners and our children and our family. We need one another.

So in addition to your date nights, or instead of them if you're single, carve out time to spend with your ladyloves, as my dear friend Meggan Watterson refers to us as, and your guy friends too, if you have close ones. When you're filled up from spending time with your friends, you'll be a better mother, partner, boss, daughter, community member, employee, and/or all of the other things you are as a woman. Spending time with other women who bolster your energy makes you a better woman. Period.

It Takes Work, and It's Worth It

Anyone who's been in a partnership for more than six months knows that it takes work to make it work. And it's worth it. When you acknowledge your part in what's not working, are willing to do the inner work to help the relationship thrive, and open up the lines of communication so that logistics run more smoothly in your partnership and family, you'll find that the little weekly investments add up to a huge load of connection, collaboration, and peace that will require so much less cleanup from miscommunication!

experiment

13

surrender

It was 3 A.M. the night of Valentine's Day. We had an extremely itchy, upset five-month-old in a Pack 'n Play around the corner in our very large hotel room, and she wouldn't stop crying and go the F to sleep. Mike went to pick her up and rock her, and I lost it.

He was breaking the rules. We were only supposed to put a hand on her chest briefly and shush her and then leave her for about a minute and then come back and do it again until she fell asleep on her own.

I had clung so tightly to the sleep consultant's rules since Penelope was 12 weeks old. They were my life raft in the sea of new motherhood, baby eczema, postpartum anxiety and insomnia, and a baby who just wasn't a sleeper.

I was so desperate for a small shred of control in a life that looked so unfamiliar to me that I was hanging on to the sleep rules for dear life and had completely lost touch with my mothering instincts, my sense of trust in my daughter to do what her body needed to do, and my belief in anyone else around me to do the right thing with our baby.

I had taken a one-way trip to crazy town and it landed me yelling at my husband at 3 A.M. for picking our screaming child up to comfort her.

This was a mothering low point.

I don't remember exactly when I finally released my grip on the sleep rules and surrendered to the reality that we had a sick kid whose profound discomfort and subsequent erratic sleep patterns could not be eradicated by perfectly following a set of rules a woman I'd never met in person who had never met our child came up with and sent to me in an e-mail attachment. But I know that when I let my fingers relax and let that piece of paper fall into the recycling bin and stopped logging Penelope's every behavior regarding sleep that my life and my marriage improved dramatically. And so did my mothering.

There are these things we want so desperately to be different than they are so we seek every possible solution. We want so badly for it to be possible to meld the world to our will and make it the sparkly version that we always had in our minds. We want to be able to fix things.

And if you're anything like me, sometimes you get yourself so rooted in a particular set of rules to the point of dogma, channeling all of your distress and worry and sadness and fear into perfection. Because if you make it about following the rules, you don't have to feel how hard it is to be responsible for the well-being of these little people who you signed up to mother.

The sleep training rules weren't the first time I'd hijacked my inner knowing to follow someone else's prescription. I'd done it with at least a half a dozen different food programs and a few fitness regimes, not to mention some advice from psychics or therapists here and there and a business strategy or two. But never with the utmost desperation of the sleep rules. And never to the extent that I was trying to control every other person in my environment as well as myself, like in this case.

If we just do exactly what the sleep coach says, our baby will sleep. That's what she said. One slipup, though, and all of our efforts are completely ruined. No deviating from the plan. The plan is my salvation. The plan is my sanity. I'm drowning here, and the plan is my only access to oxygen.

Here's what I know to be true that I forgot for a few months of insanity: There is no one set of rules that will work for every person in every situation. Our inner guidance is the best leader we have. Don't follow anything unless it's been run through your inner guidance first and it's been deemed a fit for you and your unique, beautiful mishmash of circumstances, preferences, and soul qualities.

Here's what else I know to be true: Trying to control everyone and everything around us is not only impossible, it's exhausting.

The constant worry of whether or not Mike or another caregiver was following the rules perfectly when I left Penelope was digging me deeper into the hole of exhaustion than I was already standing. I didn't need another thing to manage. If I trusted these people enough to care for my child, I needed to trust them enough to figure out how to get her to sleep and to know when to throw in the towel and just follow her cues rather than the rules this lady had come up with having no knowledge of Penelope's central nervous system or sleep cycles, or the needs of her little body.

What's so awesome about children is that they come into the world with their own rhythms and needs and cycles that we don't need to program them with. They come in complete. It's not our job to fix or finish them. It's our job to listen to them and support them (and, of course, provide adequate boundaries so that they feel safe and are safe).

My few-month trip to sleep training crazy town was the ultimate example of living out the illusion of control. And it's the illusion of control that sucks so much of our vital time and energy from our lives that could really be better invested elsewhere.

We can get psychoanalytical with ourselves and identify all of the ways we felt unsafe as children to point to why we reach for control as a coping mechanism in the first place. I've spent some time doing this (and I continue to do so with my awesome therapist and coach), and I highly recommend it because the benefits of healing your original wounds are so vast it would take me an entire other book to describe them.

However, if you're looking for a shortcut because you're not in therapy right now, don't feel like you have the time, or don't feel like you have the money to work with someone, here it is: *Stop trying to control everything.*

Instead, here are some of the things that we can control:

- How much and how deeply we breathe
- What we do or don't put in our mouths
- The words that come out of our mouths
- If and when we move our bodies
- How we respond to situations going on in our lives
- Our emotional regulation related to said situations
- What we put our attention on
- Our intentions
- Our own actions

Here are some of the things we can't control:

- The actions of others
- Other peoples' intentions

- All of the situations in our lives in their totality
- What other people say
- What other people feel
- Our children's destiny

My friend Kris Carr has a great quote: "The only time we can change another person is when they're in diapers." And even when they're in diapers, one of the only things you can change is their diapers. Who they are is pretty much who they are, no matter what their age.

Now would be a good time to look inside and ask yourself:

- *What am I trying to control right now that's not something that's actually within my realm of control?*

- *What could I stop doing that would allow me to reclaim my power and my energy to invest in things I actually have control over?*

- *What would it feel like to surrender in this area?*

If anyone had asked me these questions while I was deep in sleep coaching perfectionism, I would have immediately known, though I may not have wanted to admit, that the area I was trying to control that I needed to let go of was my daughter's sleep. I basically was spending every waking moment obsessing about it and planning out how I could execute the sleep plan perfectly or get Mike or our nanny to. It sucked up A LOT of time and energy, and in the end, what worked way better than the sleep plan was comforting our baby girl when she needed comforting, letting go of my rigidity around the whole thing, and allowing her to follow her own timing.

(It took until she was 19 months old for her to sleep through the night consistently despite night weaning her at 11 months old and despite us trying at least seven different sleep coaching techniques. And you know what? If I had it to do all over again, I would take all of the time I spent reading sleep books, hiring coaches, explaining the programs to Mike and our babysitters, and obsessing over the programs myself and just taken some really long naps. She was going to do what she was going to do, and I could have let go a lot earlier.)

When we release our control over the people and situations in our lives that are really outside of our control anyway, we not only reclaim our power and energy, we give a huge shout-out to the cosmic forces that communicates:

Hey! I believe in you! I trust that there's something going on here that's bigger than me. I know you've got this and I don't have to micromanage everything. Thanks so much for being on my side and doing all of the things you do to support me. I'm going to go back to being human now and focusing on my side of the sidewalk and doing the best I can in my arena. I trust the higher plan here. Thanks!

When we're strong-arming life all the time, it edges out support that might be available to us if we would surrender even 10 percent more.

What do you do when you see a woman who seems like she has it all together? You assume she has it all together and offer your assistance elsewhere.

What do you do when you see a woman trying to control every area of her life with a level of intensity that makes smoke come out of her ears? You cross the street and let her go about her business because ain't nothing good going to come of trying to wiggle yourself into her closed bubble of a system called the illusion of control. She's not available for help, and you're just going to get pummeled. (You can just ask my husband what it was like living with me during those months of sleep training to find out what it feels like to try to help a controlling woman. *No bueno.*)

Do you want to be either one of these types of women?

No. Because being these types of women is lonely. These types of women are making it harder than it needs to be. They're missing out on the miracles that come from letting go and letting other people in. They're missing out on the wonder that comes from letting things unfold on their own.

You know what I've learned? When I let go of how I think it should be, it often ends up way better than I could have ever possibly imagined.

If you need help with this area, I recommend getting the following tattooed on your forehead:

God,

Grant me the serenity to accept the things I cannot change,

The courage to change the things I can,

And the wisdom to know the difference.

It's called the Serenity Prayer, and it's walked a lot of big-hearted people out of their dark nights of the soul and right into the light. I'm one of them, and you can be too.

14

the final experiment:
let it be enough

While I make nearly my whole living thanks to the Internet and the ease of disseminating information near and far, the amount of information that we have available at our fingertips is super awesome and super not, all at the same time.

First of all, there are the people on the Internet. The people who adjust their photos to make their lives (and their faces and bodies) look "just so" in order to portray a version of their reality that's really not reality at all. There are the moms who make gorgeous, healthy, homemade food in cool designs for their kids. While having perfect makeup. And perky bums. And great hair. And tidy homes. With charming throw pillows.

Or the moms whose bellies are flat within weeks of giving birth. Or the families whose kitchen counters are completely clear. Like really nothing on them on a normal day of the week. Like they actually keep them that way, because you've stopped by unannounced and seen it in person, so you know. Or the couples who have sex all the time even though they've been married for 12+ years. Or the friend who looks incredibly chic no matter what time of the day it is, no matter what she's doing, and no matter how long the flight she just got off of was.

Instead of comparing ourselves to people on the Internet and finding ourselves lacking, reading all of the studies and deciding we should be doing more for our jobs, our partners, our kids, our homes, our communities, and our families, or following all of the self-help advice and jamming our lives so full of improvements that we don't have any space to enjoy our so-called improved-upon life, it's time to *let it be enough.*

Our obsession with thinking we need to do and be more shows up most acutely in our work lives and in our mothering, in my experience.

We've been brainwashed into thinking that the way to be valuable is to always go the extra mile, to always put in more hours, to always put in more effort, to always do more at work. But hopefully by now you're seeing why more isn't always better and how deliberately using breaks, cycles, and pulling back can actually lead to the same, if not better, results (not to mention preserving your well-being).

And the pressure to show up more and more as a parent and to drown our children in love, attention, and activities could bring even the strongest of mothers to her knees with feelings of inadequacy and wondering if she's really doing enough.

I discovered, first by accident and later on purpose, that doing less really is the path to greater results and well-being in my work life. All of the data I shared with you in Chapter 1 and the different Do Less Experiments peppered throughout this book have given you a pretty good case for that.

When we start to manage our energy more efficiently, give ourselves breaks, and lean into the natural ebbs and flows of the cycle of creativity and we're validated with more clients, better reviews, getting more done, or making more money, it becomes easier to adopt doing less as a way of life at work (though it does require a vigilance to dismantle the programming that still runs the vast majority of our work culture: that more will always be better).

But what about when it comes to mothering? It's not like work or a business, where there are results like increased customer retention or net revenue to prove to you that what you're doing is working. The feeling of it never being enough can be more pervasive when it comes to being a mother because there's no scorecard and everything changes all the time.

I read an article the other day that was absolute salve to my overachieving soul. It highlighted several studies that proved that essentially kids get just as much, if not more, benefit from the day-to-day time we spend with them making dinner, going to the grocery store, and doing drop-off and pickup as they do from "uninterrupted, unstressed, superfocused" time that we have this idea is supposed to be totally focused on their interests rather than our own.

One longitudinal study cited in the article actually didn't show any relationship between a child's emotional well-being, behavior, or academic performance and the amount of time their parents spent with them, between the ages of 3 to 11.[1] (The study, of course, didn't discount the importance of family meals or one-on-one time. Also, interestingly enough, in adolescence this changes and more time spent with a mother actually decreases delinquent behavior.)

Another study cited mentioned that the degree to which fathers enjoy parenting has a far greater impact on decreasing behavioral issues at school than the amount of time fathers spend with their kids. If this research isn't a vote for quality over quantity, I don't know what is.

But then we have to define quality. Quality time, according to these researchers, doesn't need to be expensive, doesn't need to be super special, and doesn't need to be some magical activity focused on your kid's interests only. Quality time could be peeling potatoes and genuinely listening to your kid talk about their day. It could be 15 minutes when they get home from school where you put your phone and computer away and sit down with them for a snack and you're actually fully with them. It could be stopping what you're doing and making full eye contact when your kid comes in to ask you a question.

Our full presence is the greatest gift we can give anyone, especially our kids. And it's not the amount of time that anyone will remember, it's the way they felt when they were with you because you were really with them. Our gift to our children is not actually our time, it's ourselves. To be fully with them when we're with them. That's all they want.

When Penelope follows me around the kitchen in the morning with her arms outstretched, saying, "Uppy, Mama, uppy!" and I stop my tornado of activity trying to get my coffee made and her fed and her lunch packed and a somewhat weather-appropriate outfit on her long enough to pick her up and watch the construction guys working across the street or do her Barbie's hair in "two ponies" as she's requested, more often than not within a few minutes she's off and ready for the next thing and I can go back to keeping the morning train moving out the door.

When I resist her, though, her need for my presence just escalates. She clings to my leg, she starts to cry, sometimes she completely unravels into a puddle on the floor. And then the kitchen is so full of drama that I can't get anything done anyway and all of our central nervous systems are suddenly on high alert. Hello, adrenaline!

More often than not she wants to be with me for a few minutes. That's it. That's all she's looking for. She's not asking me to read 20 books with her on the floor and do a craft project and for us to bake gluten-free, vegan, sugar-free cookies together that I found on Pinterest.

Nope. She's saying, *Hey, Mama! I'm here. You're here. Let's be really together for a minute. And then I'll be done.* She's not keeping track of how many minutes or hours we're spending together. But her little body and her emotions know when I'm really there and when I'm actually not. And when I'm actually not really there, she's left craving more because she might have gotten the presence of my body in a room with her, but she didn't actually get me.

Some days the meme that the best thing for a kid is to be home all day every day with her mother flies in and attaches itself to me. I start feeling guilty for the fact that she's in day care four days a week and that some weeks I want her there five days. (Though I don't feel as guilty lately because of the research I shared with you in this book that shows that kids of working mothers are just as happy as, if not happier than, kids of stay-at-home moms.)

Then I remember that she loves her friends and she asks to go to day care even on the weekends. And then I remember that I'm way happier when I'm working and thus way more able to be present with her when I'm with her because my cup is filled more often than it would be if I were home with her all day. (And, by the way, so is hers.)

I remember that when I stop making coffee in the morning and sit on the kitchen floor with her and we simply breathe together as she eats a bowl of grapes or when she asks to lie against my arm and we spend three minutes cuddling on the couch together before she's hopped off to go play with her dolls, it's enough.

It's more than enough, in fact. Showing up is all that's ever been asked of us by anyone (or anything) that matters. The power of our full presence. Actually being where we are.

The rest of it is just accessorizing, just keeping ourselves occupied and entertained while we're here for this spin on earth, however many rotations around the sun this trip might be.

Let the amount you've moved your body this week be enough.

Let the effort you put into that project be enough.

Let the amount of time you spent really truly being with your kids be enough. (They're not tracking the minutes, I promise. They just want you to be all the way there when you're there.)

Let the amount of sex you're having be enough.

Let the love you have to give be enough.

The obsession with more, with needing to be and do more, distracts us from being and doing the things we're already being and doing with all of ourselves. The mantle of disapproval we wear when we're doing or being something that we think we should be doing or being more or better takes away from the very thing we're doing or being to begin with. Obsessing about being and doing more has the opposite effect we think it will: It takes away from our actions and our presence instead of adding to them.

Have you ever worked with someone who's so convinced that they're not good enough that though their work is actually really good, their aura of lack makes working with them kind of a drag? Their obsession with not being enough manifests in them not being enough. When you stop trying to prove your value through doing, you'll find the freedom to be all of you.

The world doesn't need you busy. The world needs you here. And it's enough.

Do less. Let it be enough. And, as a result, enjoy the miraculous experience of being more of who you are.

appendix

daily energy tracker

This tracker is for you to use in whatever way feels good. Fill in as much or as little as you want at the end of each day before bed.

Date:	Day and phase of your cycle:									
🌙 Lunar Phase and/or Relevant Astrological Transits:	✏️ How was your energy today?									
	1	2	3	4	5	6	7	8	9	10
💤 How was your sleep last night?	NOTES:									

😊 How are you doing today emotionally?

🚽 How did you feel in your body today? Any symptoms to note? (Cramps, bloating, cravings)

🖥️ What did you work on today? How did that go?

✓ What went really great today?

✗ What didn't go so great?

♡ What are you grateful for today?	✏️ Is there anything else you want to make note of?

B

daily renewable planner

Date:

_____

12pm
11am
1pm
10am
2pm
9am
3pm
8am
4pm
7am
5pm
6am
6pm
5am
7pm
4am
8pm
3am
9pm
2am
10pm
1am
11pm
12am

katenorthrup.com

resources

Here's a list of other resources to continue your do less journey. Deprogramming ourselves from the belief that our worth is dependent upon what we do is an ongoing journey, and these tools will help you as you continue this important work.

Free Do Less Support Bundle

www.katenorthrup.com/gifts

Origin Collective

Join my membership for entrepreneurial women who are actively practicing having more by doing less in their daily lives. Get monthly tools, resources, strategy, and support. Go to www.origincollective.com/doless for exclusive enrollment for Do Less readers.

OTHER PROGRAMS

Go to www.katenorthrup.com/shop for a current list of programs, products, and events that I'm offering to go deeper with this work.

BOOKS

Women's Health

Women's Bodies, Women's Wisdom by Christiane Northrup, M.D.

The Fourth Trimester: A Postpartum Guide to Healing Your Body, Balancing Your Emotions, and Restoring Your Vitality by Kimberly Ann Johnson

WomanCode: Perfect Your Cycle, Amplify Your Fertility, Supercharge Your Sex Drive, and Become a Power Source by Alisa Vitti

Parenting

The Awakened Family: How to Raise Empowered, Resilient, and Conscious Children by Dr. Shefali Tsabary

Mothering From Your Center: Tapping Your Body's Natural Energy for Pregnancy, Birth, and Parenting by Tami Lynn Kent

Simplicity Parenting: Using the Extraordinary Power of Less to Raise Calmer, Happier, and More Secure Kids by Kim John Payne and Lisa M. Ross

Decluttering

The Life-Changing Magic of Tidying Up: The Japanese Art of Decluttering and Organizing by Marie Kondo

Business/Money/Success

The 4-Hour Workweek: Escape 9–5, Live Anywhere, and Join the New Rich by Tim Ferriss

Sacred Success: A Course in Financial Miracles by Barbara Stanny

The Big Leap: Conquer Your Hidden Fear and Take Life to the Next Level by Gay Hendricks

Drop the Ball: Achieve More by Doing Less by Tiffany Dufu

Essentialism: The Disciplined Pursuit of Less by Greg McKeown

The One Thing: The Surprisingly Simple Truth Behind Extraordinary Results by Gary Keller and Jay Papasan

Social Justice/Social Change

Emergent Strategy: Shaping Change, Changing Worlds by Adrienne Maree Brown

OTHER

Own Your Glow: A Soulful Guide to Luminous Living and Crowing the Queen Within by Latham Thomas

Feminine Genius: The Provocative Path to Waking Up and Turning On the Wisdom of Being a Woman by LiYana Silver

Daring to Rest: Reclaim Your Power with Yoga Nidra Rest Meditation by Karen Brody

You Have 4 Minutes to Change Your Life: Simple 4-Minute Meditations for Inspiration, Transformation, and True Bliss by Rebekah Borucki

endnotes

Introduction

1. Roddy Scheer and Doug Moss, "Dirt Poor: Have Fruits and Vegetables Become Less Nutritious?" *Scientific American*, accessed July 11, 2018, https://www.scientificamerican.com/article/soil-depletion-and-nutrition-loss.

2. "Stress Nutrition Basics," California Earth Minerals Corporation, accessed July 19, 2018, http://www.californiaearthminerals.com/stress_nutrition_basics.html.

3. Micha Kaufman, "Glass Ceilings Smashed by Freelancing Moms," *Forbes*, May 9, 2014, https://www.forbes.com/sites/michakaufman/2014/05/09/glass-ceiling-smashed-by-freelancing-moms/#5c66867d5790.

4. Gretchen Livingston, "Among 41 Nations, U.S. Is the Outlier When It Comes to Paid Parental Leave," Pew Research Center, September 26, 2016, http://www.pewresearch.org/fact-tank/2016/09/26/u-s-lacks-mandated-paid-parental-leave.

5. Ibid.

6. Tiffany Dufu, *Drop the Ball: Achieving More by Doing Less*, New York: Flatiron Books, 2017.

Chapter 1

1. Mika Kivimaki, Ph.D., et al., "Long Working Hours and Risk of Coronary Heart Disease and Stroke," *The Lancet* 386, no. 10005, (October 15, 2015): 1739–46, http://www.thelancet.com/journals/lancet/article/PIIS0140-6736(15)60295-1/abstract.

2. Chris Isadore and Tami Luhby, "Turns Out Americans Work Really Hard . . . but Some Want to Work Harder," *@CNNMoney,* July 9, 2015, http://money.cnn.com/2015/07/09/news/economy/americans-work-bush/index.html.

3. Travis Bradberry, Ph.D., "Stress Literally Shrinks Your Brain (7 Ways to Reverse This Effect)," *Huffington Post,* last modified December 6, 2017, https://www.huffingtonpost.com/dr-travis-bradberry/stress-literally-shrinks_b_11353274.html.

4. K. Anders Ericsson, Michael J. Prietula, and Edward T. Cokely, "The Making of an Expert," *Harvard Business Review,* July–August 2007 issue, accessed July 18, 2018, https://hbr.org/2007/07/the-making-of-an-expert.

5. Alina Vrabie, "The Science Behind Concentration and Improved Focus," *Sandglaz Blog Archive,* December 6, 2013, http://blog.sandglaz.com/the-science-behind-concentration/.

6. Travis Bradberry, Ph.D., "Multitasking Damages Your Brain and Career, New Studies Suggest," *Forbes,* October 8, 2014, https://www.forbes.com/sites/travisbradberry/2014/10/08/multitasking-damages-your-brain-and-career-new-studies-suggest/#12f06caa56ee.

7. Travis Bradberry, Ph.D., "Here's How Much Work Your Brain Can Handle Before Needing a Break," *Business Insider,* January 5, 2016, http://www.businessinsider.com/this-is-the-perfect-amount-of-time-to-work-each-day-2016-1.

8. Bec Crew, "Sweden Is Shifting to a 6-Hour Work Day," *Science Alert,* September 30, 2015, http://www.sciencealert.com/sweden-is-shifting-to-a-6-hour-workday.

9. Denis Campbell, "UK Needs Four-Day Week to Combat Stress, Says Top Doctor," *The Guardian,* July 1, 2014, https://www.theguardian.com/society/2014/jul/01/uk-four-day-week-combat-stress-top-doctor.

10. Jason Fried, "Be More Productive. Take Time Off," *The New York Times,* August 18, 2012, http://www.nytimes.com/2012/08/19/opinion/sunday/be-more-productive-shorten-the-workweek.html.

11. Charlotte Graham-McLay, "A 4-Day Workweek? A Test Run Shows a Surprising Result," *The New York Times,* July 19, 2018, https://www.nytimes.com/2018/07/19/world/asia/four-day-workweek-new-zealand.html.

12. Maria Konnikova, "Why Not a Three-Day Week?" *The New Yorker*, August 5, 2014, https://www.newyorker.com/science/maria-konnikova/three-day-week.

13. Aaron Taube, "6 Arguments for a Shorter Workweek," *Business Insider*, September 1, 2014, http://www.businessinsider.com/arguments-for-the-four-day-workweek-2014-8.

14. Hazel Sheffield, "Mexico's Richest Man Carlos Slim Says We May Soon Have a Three-Day Workweek," *Independent*, August 5, 2016, http://www.independent.co.uk/news/business/news/carlos-slim-mexico-three-day-work-week-six-hour-day-telmex-america-movil-productivity-a7173501.html.

Chapter 2

1. Melanie Axelrod, "Men Can Smell Fertility, Study Says," *ABC News*, April 5, 2001, http://abcnews.go.com/Health/story?id=117526.

2. Peter Grossenbacher, "What Is Synesthesia," Naropa University (blog), accessed July 19, 2018, http://www.naropa.edu/academics/consciousness-lab/what-is-synesthesia.php.

3. Clare N. Jonas and Mark C. Price, "Not All Synesthetes Are Alike: Spatial vs. Visual Dimensions of Sequence-Space Synesthesia," *Frontiers in Psychology*, October 30, 2014, https://www.frontiersin.org/articles/10.3389/fpsyg.2014.01171/full.

Chapter 3

1. Sarah Knapton, "Why Winter Is a Mental Struggle: Human Brain More Active in Summer, Scientists Find," *The Telegraph*, February 8, 2016, http://www.telegraph.co.uk/news/science/science-news/12147075/Why-winter-is-a-mental-struggle-human-brain-more-active-in-summer-scientists-find.html.

Chapter 4

1. Ferris Jabr, "How Human Eggs Woo Sperm," *New Scientist*, March 16, 2011, https://www.newscientist.com/article/mg20928043-400-how-human-eggs-woo-sperm/.

Experiment #1

1. Cecilia Tasca, et al., "Women and Hysteria in the History of Mental Health," *Clinical Practice and Epidemiology in Mental Health* 8 (October 19, 2012): 110–119, https://www.ncbi.nlm.nih.gov/pmc/articles/PMC3480686.

Experiment #3

1. Lori Haase, et al., "When the brain does not adequately feel the body: Links between low resilience and interoception," *Biological Psychology* 116 (January 2016): 37–45, https://www.ncbi.nlm.nih.gov/pubmed/26607442.

Experiment #5

1. Darcia Narvaez, Ph.D., "New Moms Need Social Support," *Psychology Today*, January 13, 2013, https://www.psychologytoday.com/blog/moral-landscapes/201301/new-moms-need-social-support.

2. Jenny McLeish and Maggie Redshaw, "Mothers' Accounts of the Impact on Emotional Well-being of Organised Peer Support in Pregnancy and Early Parenthood: A Qualitative Study," *BMC Pregnancy Childbirth*, January 13, 2017, https://www.ncbi.nlm.nih.gov/pmc/articles/PMC5237175.

Experiment #6

1. Liz Mineo, "Good Genes Are Nice, But Joy Is Better," *The Harvard Gazette*, April 11, 2017, https://news.harvard.edu/gazette/story/2017/04/over-nearly-80-years-harvard-study-has-been-showing-how-to-live-a-healthy-and-happy-life.

Experiment #9

1. "Adolescent Sleep Needs and Patterns: Research Report and Resource Guide," National Sleep Foundation, accessed July 18, 2018, https://sleepfoundation.org/sites/default/files/sleep_and_teens_report1.pdf.

2. Nikhil Swaminathan, "Can a Lack of Sleep Cause Psychiatric Disorders?" *Scientific American*, October 23, 2007, https://www.scientificamerican.com/article/can-a-lack-of-sleep-cause.

3. Brian Palmer, "Can You Die from Lack of Sleep?" *Slate*, May 11, 2009, http://www.slate.com/articles/news_and_politics/explainer/2009/05/can_you_die_from_lack_of_sleep.html.

4. Laura Schocker, "Here's a Horrifying Picture of What Sleep Loss Will Do to You," *Huffington Post*, last modified December 6, 2017, https://www.huffingtonpost.com/2014/01/08/sleep-deprivation_n_4557142.html.

5. Markham Heid, "What's the Best Time to Sleep?" *TIME*, last modified July 19 2016, http://time.com/3183183/best-time-to-sleep.

6. "Blue Light Has a Dark Side," *Harvard Health Letter* (blog), last modified December 30, 2017, https://www.health.harvard.edu/staying-healthy/blue-light-has-a-dark-side.

Experiment #10

1. John Brandon, "The Surprising Reason Millennials Check Their Phones 150 Times a Day," *Inc.*, April 17, 2017, https://www.inc.com/john-brandon/science-says-this-is-the-reason-millennials-check-their-phones-150-times-per-day.html.

2. Kermit Pattison, "Worker, Interrupted: The Cost of Task Switching," *Fast Company*, July 28, 2008, https://www.fastcompany.com/944128/worker-interrupted-cost-task-switching.

3. Bob Sullivan and Hugh Thompson, "Brain Interrupted," *The New York Times*, May 3, 2013, https://www.nytimes.com/2013/05/05/opinion/sunday/a-focus-on-distraction.html.

Experiment #14

1. Lila MacLellan, "Research Shows Daily Family Life Is All the 'Quality Time' Kids Need," *Quartz at Work*, November 5, 2017, https://work.qz.com/1099307/research-shows-daily-family-life-is-all-the-quality-time-kids-need.

acknowledgments

As with any creative endeavor, I don't believe any of us is solely responsible for bringing an idea into manifestation. Just as it takes a village to raise a child (at least, ideally), it takes a village to get a book done! It's my pleasure to take a pause and honor the village that helped bring this book into the world.

Thank you to the whole team at Hay House for continuing to bug me about a second book, even though I kept saying no. Your persistence means the world to me. A special thank-you to Patti Gift, Sally Mason-Swaab, and Nicolette Young for being an editorial dream team. (Also thank you to the cosmos for the synchronicity that Sally, Nicolette, and I were all pregnant during the creation process of this book. This divine wink was not lost on me.)

Thank you, Lisa Fraley, my dear friend and lawyer, for helping me iron out the contract.

Thank you to Julia Nickles, one of my most favorite #wordnerds, not to mention one of the smartest, most talented women I know, for compiling a great deal of the supporting data to prove to us all that doing less does, in fact, bring you more, and for being such an enthusiastic early reader.

Thank you to the Maine Rockstars, a group of women I've met with monthly to mastermind, hold space, share ideas, get feedback, and simply love for the past four years: Carrie Montgomery, Christina Neuner, Laura Thompson Brady, Amber Lilyestrom, Lisa Fraley, and Licia Morelli.

There is no way I could have had the bandwidth to write this book if it weren't for the incredible team of people running our company who I have the honor of working with. Thank you to Hayley Lachambre, Joe Scoppino, Lisa Fiorvante, Akilah Pitts, Brandi Bernoskie, TaKisha August, Mary Quinn, Julia Nickles, and Matt Mawhinney for keeping the gears moving in our business every day, for showing up with tremendous love, and for being so darn smart and talented.

Licia Morelli, I don't know what I did to deserve a woman like you, not only as a friend, but also to lead our company. You are wise, proactive, organized, compassionate, brilliant, funny, and loyal. You keep it ALL together, and there's no way in hell I would have been able to write this book without your support and brilliant insight.

To the people who've inspired the Do Less way, I'm so grateful for you for being trailblazers. Whether I know you personally or not, you have been mentors to me. My everlasting thanks to: Barbara Stanny, Kimberly Johnson, Latham Thomas, Molly Caro May, Tami Lynn Kent, Adrienne Maree Brown, Alisa Vitti, Karen Brody, Sarah Kathleen Peck, Jennifer Racioppi, LiYana Silver, Greg McKeown, Tim Ferriss, Stu McLaren, James Wedmore, and Tiffany Dufu.

To Meggan Watterson, our voice memos back and forth as we both welcomed our next books into the world saved me. Being "pregnant" with you is my favorite, as is being your ladylove.

Sarah Jenks, our phone conversations around motherhood and entrepreneurship planted the seed for this book. If it weren't for you asking me how to actually do less, I don't know that this book would exist. Thank you.

Liz Long, Ellen Folan, Hannah Magee, Abagael Baldwin, Sarah Tangredi, Deborah Kern, Andrea Coles, Eliza Reynolds, Rachel Northrup, and Noah Levy: Thank you for believing in me, for being incredible, lifelong friends (and family), and for cheering me on always, especially around this book.

Erin Stutland and Laura Garnett: our chats about books and babies helped so much with navigating the unique dynamic of caring for infants while publishing a book. Thank you both.

Anne Davin, your insights, guidance, and coaching helped me transform in ways that this project required of me, and I'm so grateful for your support.

To the beautiful caretakers at YDC, thank you for caring for our girls in the beautiful way that you do, so that I can show up for my work outside motherhood undistracted and knowing that my girls are in safe hands.

Emilia McClellan, thank you for taking incredible care of our girls, our home, and our bellies so that I have the energy to care for our business and my ideas.

I'm so grateful for the Empresses of Origin for answering my call to reimagine motherhood and entrepreneurship and for contributing your ideas and experience so generously to this book.

Bill and Michele Watts: Thank you for raising such an incredible man to be my husband and to be the father of our girls and also for your trips out east to hang with the grand-babies so I could shut my office door and jam on this book.

Dad, Tracey, and Waverly, thank you for playing with Penelope, holding Ruby, making dinner for us, and simply being there. You are a crucial piece of our village, and we're so grateful.

Diane Grover, you will ever remain a beacon for me of how to run a business with integrity, professionalism, and heart.

Thank you for answering my questions within moments, for loving my girls, for taking incredible care of my mama, and for being there all these years.

To my dear sister, Ann Moller, I don't know if anyone in the world believes in me more than you do. Our conversations around the Renewable Planner system, energy management, and our cyclical nature as women have been invaluable to me in better understanding this work and in making it real for the rest of the world. I love you to the moon and back.

To my mother, Christiane Northrup, M.D., thank you for blazing the trail so that I could take the baton and birth this next iteration of our maternal legacy's work. Watching you unravel your programming to always do more gave me permission to do the same and to carry on the message of teaching women to care for their exquisite selves as a means of making the world a better place. Thank you for every conversation we had that helped birth this book and, of course, for birthing me.

To my incredible husband and partner in life, parenting, and business, Mike Watts, there is no way I could do less, or really do anything, without you. The way you show up for me and the girls is one of the most healing, beautiful things I've ever witnessed. You are everything.

To Penelope and Ruby, my daughters, for teaching me through simply being who you are that it's our presence, not our accomplishments, that truly matter. I love you both beyond words, and I'm so grateful you chose me to be your mama. This work wouldn't exist without you both.

And, finally, to all the women who mother, whether you've given birth biologically or not: You are the heartbeat of humanity. Never, ever forget how important you are. Without you none of us would even be here being or doing anything. You are the origin. Never forget it.

about the author

Kate Northrup is an entrepreneur who supports ambitious women to light up the world without burning themselves out in the process. She is the founder and CEO of Origin® Collective, a membership where women all over the world gather to achieve more while doing less. Her first book, *Money: A Love Story*, has been published in five languages. Kate lives with her husband and business partner, Mike, and their two daughters in Maine.

Hay House Titles of Related Interest

YOU CAN HEAL YOUR LIFE, the movie,
starring Louise Hay & Friends
(available as a 1-DVD program, an expanded 2-DVD set,
and an online streaming video)
Learn more at www.hayhouse.com/louise-movie

THE SHIFT, the movie,
starring Dr. Wayne W. Dyer
(available as a 1-DVD program, an expanded 2-DVD set,
and an online streaming video)
Learn more at www.hayhouse.com/the-shift-movie

***

LUCKY BITCH: A Guide for Exceptional Women to Create Outrageous Success, by Denise Duffield-Thomas

RISE SISTER RISE: A Guide to Unleashing the Wise, Wild Woman Within, by Rebecca Campbell

SHE MEANS BUSINESS: Turn Your Ideas into Reality and Become a Wildly Successful Entrepreneur, by Carrie Green

WOMEN ROCKING BUSINESS: The Ultimate Step-by-Step Guidebook to Create a Thriving Life Doing Work You Love, by Sage Lavine

WORTHY: Boost Your Self-Worth to Grow Your Net Worth, by Nancy Levin

All of the above are available at your local bookstore, or may be ordered by contacting Hay House (see next page).

We hope you enjoyed this Hay House book. If you'd like to receive our online catalog featuring additional information on Hay House books and products, or if you'd like to find out more about the Hay Foundation, please contact:

Hay House, Inc., P.O. Box 5100, Carlsbad, CA 92018-5100
(760) 431-7695 or (800) 654-5126
(760) 431-6948 (fax) or (800) 650-5115 (fax)
www.hayhouse.com® • www.hayfoundation.org

———

Published in Australia by:
Hay House Australia Pty. Ltd., 18/36 Ralph St., Alexandria NSW 2015
Phone: 612-9669-4299 • *Fax:* 612-9669-4144 • www.hayhouse.com.au

Published in the United Kingdom by:
Hay House UK, Ltd., Astley House, 33 Notting Hill Gate, London W11 3JQ
Phone: 44-20-3675-2450 • *Fax:* 44-20-3675-2451 • www.hayhouse.co.uk

Published in India by: Hay House Publishers India,
Muskaan Complex, Plot No. 3, B-2, Vasant Kunj, New Delhi 110 070
Phone: 91-11-4176-1620 • *Fax:* 91-11-4176-1630 • www.hayhouse.co.in

———

Access New Knowledge.
Anytime. Anywhere.

Learn and evolve at your own pace
with the world's leading experts.

www.hayhouseU.com

6/7/19

I've shamed, hated mistrust
my body. In our culture we
as women are taught to
do that. To look in return
of hate. Selves.

And now I really saw

wrong + feel how all these
years I treated myself
w/ hate. For others - b/c I bought
into the collective -
But at my expense.

And now I wonder,
am I too late - is it too
late? All this pain
a manifestation of a
lifetime of _hate_ to my
body / myself. Can I
heal + ~~take~~ rewrite
my relat to my body?